CHEF GABRIELE A. NICOLETTI

50 Recipes & glass of Wine

RECIPES AND TEXT
CHEF GABRIELE A. NICOLETTI

WINE CONSULTANT
NICOLETTA NICOLETTI

GENERAL EDITOR
STUDIO F&D - ITALY

PHOTOGRAPHS
BIG STOCK PHOTOS
LISA PLUTH

DESIGN
SAVINO D'ANDREA

WINE PROVIDED BY
WINE BANK OF SAN DIEGO, CA

NICOLETTI & NICOLETTI
PUBLISHING LIMITED 2007

United States of America

Biography
CHEF GABRIELE A. NICOLETTI

Chef Gabriel A. Nicoletti, Owner of creativechefs.com and Director of Food Service at Redwood Town Court have been creating innovative Mediterranean Italian Cuisine for more than 30 years.

Born in Italy, he began his career as a busboy in a local beach restaurant in Lido di Roma. He worked throughout Europe and his love for cooking quickly brought him to the United States in his early 20's. He began working in Los Angeles for Via Veneto café. He lived in Jamaica, where he was the Executive Chef and co-owner of Casa Blanca restaurant & supper club, Little Italy restaurant, the Pirates Pearch's and the Deep restaurant.

After many years of living abroad Chef Gabriele moved back to North America and he co-owned Zero Italian cuisine in Toronto, Canada. He also worked in New York as Manager/Chef of Café Trilussa.

In 1972 he received a Certificate in Tax Analysis in Italy and in 1986 he received his Associates Degree in Hotel and Restaurant Management in the USA. Throughout his many years of training he published a guide in Food and Beverage Management and three cookbooks.

A taste of My Italy

Buon Appetito.

50 recipes & Glass of Wine

Chef Gabriel A. Nicoletti is a Certified Master Chef and member of the National Professional Italian Association of Chefs, and Certified Executive Chef with The American Culinary Federation.

His love for the Culinary Art began at a very young age and has followed him throughout his life. His premise for good food is that each ingredient is unique and should have its own place in a dish...

CHEF GABRIELE A. NICOLETTI

Fusion Food

Fusion food has a long and noble history. Today's bold experiment is tomorrow's classic dish.

Fusion food a style of cooking, which is increasingly popular, but it seems, also increasingly controversial. Some people seem to think that ingredients from different world cuisines should never meet on the same plate.

The term 'Fusion' originated in the United States, Fusion is a term which simply implies the Fusion of several cuisines in one dish. Many chefs across the country busily scour North Africa for couscous, the Mediterranean for olives and the West Indies for plantain - ingredients.

Restaurant reviewers who criticize fusion cooking for taking ingredients from many countries and 'fusing' them on one plate might have marveled at, say, a wonderful Italian dish of braised aborigines and potatoes served with guinea fowl. Well, as any people know, aborigines originally came from China, potatoes from South America, and guinea fowl from Guinea, West Africa. Indeed, in their time, the aborigine and the potato were themselves regarded as exotic. Fusion food of a different sort.

No cuisine today can be classified, understood or ultimately appreciated by looking at borders on a modern map. Italian, Spanish and French cuisines would not be what they are today if explorers had not liked the strange foodstuffs they brought back from their voyages of discovery. The fact that potato, tomato, orange, lemon and rice all thrive in the European climate has meant that they have become part of our food culture over the centuries. If the mango or kaffir lime tree had been able to grow here, I'm sure the 18th-century cookery writer Brillat-Savarin would have come up with a recipe for them as well.

Fusion at its best allows ingredients from all over the globe to be marinated, cooked and served together in harmony on the same plate. The secret behind it is the successful combination of the familiar with newer, less well-known ingredients. Puréed green chilies and coriander can be stirred into a simple chicken stew at the last moment. Lemon grass or lemon myrtle can replace lemon zest in a seafood risotto. Coconut milk can be used to make baked custard, replacing some of the cream, altering the taste and texture delightfully.

Diners' tastes and expectations are changing rapidly. Cheap air travel means that more people are traveling to exotic parts of the world where they can experience the 'global store cupboard' for themselves. They enjoy experiencing these flavors again when they return to home shores.

It is a shame that critics are so divided over fusion food, and sad, too, that some arrive at the table armed with prejudices against anything innovative and popular. Why can't they simply relax and accept that if something makes you excited, be it galangal or coq au vin, then it is worthy of praise? No one is denying that classic dishes with traditional ingredients are fully deserving of the plaudits they receive, but no matter how brilliant and respected classical cuisine might be, cooking is a living art, which changes and develops, as do the people who are eating and preparing it. Enjoy it. Fusion food tastes good.

How Wine is Made

Grapes grow on vines. There are many different types of grapes, but the best wine grape is the European Vitis vinifera. It is considered optimal because it has the right balance of sugar and acid to create a good fermented wine without the addition of sugar or w ater. It has been said that the wine is only as good as the grape; a poor winemaker can ruin good grapes, but a good winemaker isn't going to make great wine from inferior grapes.

Now before I say anything else about grapes, let me point out an error I have made in drafts of this document (and for all I know it may persist-proofreading is an art). That is the difference between "varieties" of grapes and "varietals". The word "varietal" means "have or pertaining to a variety".

Types of grapes are "varieties". Wines made from a single variety are varietal wines. So, for example, a 100% Cabernet Sauvignon wine is a varietal. The cabernet sauvignon grape, zinfandel grape and merlot grape are varieties of grapes. (Of course, don't be confused that, for example, United States law allows a wine to be labeled C abernet Sauvignon so long as it has at least 75% of that variety of grape. Now, is that clear?).

Vines start producing grapes about three years after planting; a useable crop after five years. They reach their prime in terms of crop yield between ages ten and thirty. Vines can grow for a hundred years , though production is reduced, as they get older. However, reduced production (which is also caused in other ways--growing in poor soil, lack of irrigation , pruning the vines, climate, etc., the so-called "stressing the vines") can lead to "better" wine. So some very good wines come from "old vines".

50 Recipes & glass of Wine

How to Serve Wine

Having chosen your wine, whether for an important dinner-party, or simply self-indulgence, proper serving conditions greatly enhance its enjoyment.

Serving Temperature: Perhaps the most important aspect of wine service as it can greatly affect the taste and the aroma of the wine. White wines benefit from chilling but if left in the fridge overnight will chill to around 4°C, enough to mask all the flavor and aroma. If served at around 8-10° they will be so much better. If a wine needs to be chilled quickly, iced water is a far more effective means than placing it in a container of ice cubes. The term "room temperature" for red wines can be very misleading as it has a huge variant and in many cases is too warm anyway. Most red wines are best served at "cellar temperature" around 15-16° to embellish the flavor and lift the natural aromas. If a red wine is very cold try decanting it into a warm jug or pouring it into warm glasses. You can also use a microwave but be careful not to cook the wine - 15-20 seconds will usually suffice. Some light red fruity wines benefit from light chilling to around 10° e.g. Beaujolais, especially for summer drinking.

Opening the bottle: Remove the metal foil using a sharp knife or special foil cutter ensuring that no jagged bits remain on the pouring surface - this can cause unsightly dribbling. Most modern corkscrews are effective but invariably an old or weak cork may break or disintegrate. If it proves difficult to remove try pushing it into the bottle and decant the wine into a jug using a skewer or kebab stick to hold it down. If there are bits of cork in the wine filter it through a simple kitchen funnel using a coffee filter. Be especially careful with Champagne and Sparkling Wine as the corks can eject with tremendous force and cause injury. Always open these bottles at an angle away from you (and your best china). Remove the restraining wire and hold down the cork while twisting the bottle from the base. As the cork ejects, angle it out of the neck to release the gas "softly" - racing drivers take note - anyway, you will enjoy a lot more of your wine!

Breathing: Many people like to open serious red wines hours in advance to allow the wine to "breathe". It can be effective in removing any "bottle stink" or "mercaptans" in a wine but the best form of breathing is agitation in the glass. Decanting: A much debated subject and generally only necessary for wines which by nature of the way in which they are made, throw sediment such as Vintage Port. Decanting can help a wine to breathe or aerate. When decanting, the wine should be poured slowly and steadily into a clean glass jug or decanter. Using a candle or bright light will show the sediment as it gathers in the shoulder of the bottle.

Glasses: The simpler and plainer the better. Ideally, but not necessarily tulip shaped with a wider bowl and tapering narrow at the top. A long stem allows for ease of swirling and the glass shape will trap and deliver the aromas. Holding the glass by the stem minimizes temperature change and avoids unsightly finger marks. Many people like to serve white wine in a larger glass followed by red wine in a smaller version, which can be aesthetically very pleasing but often has little bearing on the style of wine served. You will also need more glasses.

Pouring: Never fill the glass. The half way mark is fine. It may look mean but you can pour as often as people require. It allows the wine to breathe in the glass and for the recipient to swirl the wine and enjoy the aromas. As a general rule serve white before red, young before old and keep the good wine until last. If you hold the bottle by the base and give your wrist a slight twist as you finish pouring you will avoid the dribble factor. Try it - it works!

50 Recipes & glass of Wine

Angel Hair Pasta with Shrimp & Scallops

Ingredients

- 1 cup broccoli
- 1 lb. baby pork ribs
- 1/2 lb. shrimp
- 1/2 lb. scallops
- Salt
- 1/4 cup olive oil
- 4 Tbsp. unsalted butter
- 2 scallions cut
- 1 clove garlic
- 4 Tbsp. white wine
- 1 lb. angel hair pasta
- Grated Parmesan cheese

Chef Recommended Wine

Avignonesi
Vino Nobile
di Montepulciano

DIRECTIONS

Cut Broccoli into flowerets. Cook inlightly salted boiling water for 3-4 minutes until crispy. Drain and place in ice water to cool. Drain. In a saucepan, heat oil and 3 Tbsp. butter and sauté the scallions and garlic for 2 minutes. Add the shrimp, scallops, and broccoli. Sauté all with wine for 5 minutes.

Grill baby pork ribs; brush with a light BBQ sauce and bake for 1 hour at 375º F.

Boil the angel hair pasta in a large water pot; drain and serve in a bowl.

Garnish with a sprinkle of Parmesan cheese.

Why use a Wine Decanter

Placing a wine in a decanter "wakes up" the wine so that it reveals its full personality.

Decanting either separates oxygenation of a young or tannic wine in order to release its aromas, or enables the liquid from the sediment for a vintage wine.

Decanting also presents the wine in a glass or crystal receptacle, which highlights the natural colors.

2002

Avignonesi
Vino Nobile
di Montepulciano

A good quality red with dried cherry and light chocolate aromas & flavors.
Medium to-light finish.

50 Recipes & glass of Wine

Angel Hair with Lobster & Shrimp

Ingredients

- 1/2 of a 12 oz. pkg. angel hair pasta
- 2 tbsp. butter
- 1/2 lb. large shrimp or lobster shelled & deveined
- 1 clove garlic, minced
- 1/3 cup Parmesan cheese, grated
- 1/4 cup fresh parsley, chopped
- 1 teaspoon salt
- 1/2 teaspoon coarse ground pepper

DIRECTIONS

Prepare angel hair pasta according to package directions.

In large skillet, heat olive oil and butter.

Add shrimp or lobster & garlic. Cook & stir until shrimp or lobster is opaque.

Combine hot angel hair pasta, shrimp or lobster mixture, cheese, parsley, salt & pepper.

Toss to mix. Serve immediately. Garnish with red-yellow peppers and asparagus julienne cut.

Chef Recommended Wine

Canalicchio di Sopra
Brunello di Montalcino

Grape Variety

The wine-producing vine, as we know it, or 'vitis vinifera' to give it its botanical family name, will produce and ripen fruit throughout the mainly temperate regions of the world. Broadly speaking this area lies between 30° and 50° North and 30° and 50° South of the equator. Outside these latitudes it is either too cool - grapes will not ripen fully, or too hot - grapes ripen too early with low acidity and high alcohol.

In more marginal regions where heat is great, altitude and ocean influences can have a cooling effect and likewise in some of the cooler regions, south facing slopes and proximity to water can maximize the vine's exposure to the sun. These factors are known as microclimates and can greatly influence the location of a vineyard site and the choice of variety planted.

As a general rule, grapes need a minimum of 1500 hours of sunshine to ripen fully, red more so than white, which is why you will see more white grapes planted in cooler regions such as Germany and New Zealand.

The trend towards selling varietals wines continues unabated with many countries now labeling at least some of their wines as 'Merlot', 'Chardonnay', 'Riesling' etc. Many top quality wines however, are not permitted to use varietals names because of the 'cépage' (grape mix) required by law. Red Bordeaux wines, for example, are a blend of often four different grapes including, but not exclusively, Cabernet Sauvignon and Merlot. Other equally fine wines such as red and white Burgundy are made from single grape varieties but choose, for marketing and historical reasons, to use their regional appellations. Many people have enjoyed an excellent Barolo or Chianti but have never heard of Nebbiolo or Sangiovese. Others may enjoy a nice bottle of Chablis and not realize that it is 100 per cent Chardonnay. Our varietals index is designed to tell you a little about the most popular grape varieties and to lead you to wines that include, even in part, those grapes. We hope you find this format useful.

2001

Canalicchio di Sopra Brunello di Montalcino

Medium red. Pungent dried red berries and rose complicated by mocha, leather and spices: classic perfumed sangiovese. Then suave and silky in the mouth, with lovely vinosity and length thanky to harmonious acidity. Flavors similar to the aromas. Dry, concentrated and firmly structured Brunello, with excellent mouth coverage, finegrained tannins and excellent persistence.

Apple & Pear Salad
with Pine Nuts

Ingredients

- 1 large red apple, thinly sliced
- 1 large pear, sliced thinly
- 1 large orange, peeled & sliced
- 1/3 cup vegetable oil
- 3 tablespoons white wine vinegar
- 1 tablespoon honey
- 1/2 cup pine nuts
- Spring Mix or lettuce leaves

DIRECTIONS

In a large bowl, combine sliced fruit.
In a small bowl, combine oil, vinegar & honey; blend well.

Pour oil mixture over the fruit, tossing to coat well.

Arrange fruit on 6 lettuce lined salad dishes; sprinkle each dish with a heaping teaspoon of chopped pine nuts.

Chef Recommended Wine

Chateau Montelena
Riesling (Potter Vallet)

Grape Variety

Airen

The most widely grown white grape in Spain, where it accounts for over 30 per cent of Spanish wine production primarily in the central 'La Mancha' region. Used not only for producing varietals whites but also as a blending grape for the more beefy reds of the Valdepenas region.

Aligoté

The second white grape of Burgundy and very much the 'poor relation' of Chardonnay.

Originally used as a blending wine with Chardonnay, it is now producing some interesting varietals wines thanks to stainless steel fermentation and modern vinification methods. Somewhat tart and acidic, it is considered the ideal base wine for the French aperitif, Kir.

Baga

Widely planted red grape of Portugal notably in the Bairrada region. It gives dense color and extract, is thick skinned and prolific. Not noted for fine wine production.

Barbera

Italy's most common red grape originally from the Piedmont region of the Northwest but now grown throughout the South. Has grown in popularity outside Italy notably in California and Argentina. Vigorous, high yielding grape that grows well in poor soils. Produces wines of good extract and color without the harsh tannins of its neighbor, Nebbiolo.

2002

*Chateau
Montelena
Riesling
(Potter Vallet)*

A lovely pale yellow.
Muted nose. Crisp, clean
flavor of peaches.

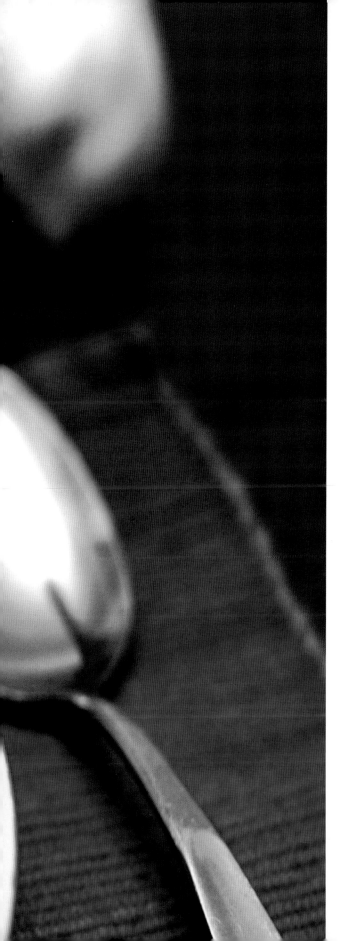

Avocado Soup

Ingredients

- 1/2 cup butter
- 1 medium onion, finely chopped
- 1 oz. fresh ginger, peeled & grated
- 1 large avocado, peeled and grated
- 2 cups chicken stock
- 1 teaspoon black pepper
- 1/2 cup light cream
- 1 scallion

DIRECTIONS

Melt the butter in a sauté pan. Cook the onions and grated ginger for about 2 minutes. Add the mashed avocado and chicken stock.

Mix all ingredients thoroughly, using a wire whisk to eliminate lumps.

Simmer slowly for about 10-15 minutes. Add salt, pepper and cream. Stir and chill for at least an hour.

Chill bowls before serving. Garnish each bowl with scallions.

Chef Recommended Wine

Joffré
Valle de Vco, Mendoza

Grape Variety

Cabernet Franc

One of the principal red grapes of Bordeaux, particularly St-Emilion, and also the dominant red varietals of the Loire Valley. Generally more stalky and greener than its noble partner Cabernet Sauvignon, it performs well in cooler regions, is resistant to disease and survives well in heavier clay soils. It provides a useful 'insurance policy' for the Bordelaise vignerons in cooler vintages. It is the primary varietals in the top Premier Grand Cru Classé, St-Emilion - 'Château Cheval Blanc. Now planted throughout Italy and in Chile as well as Australia's Clare Valley.

Cabernet Sauvignon

The classic grape of Bordeaux and the dominant variety in all the top growths of the Medoc. A most fashionable varietals, sought the world over and synonymous with rich blackcurrant concentration, cassis and cedar wood. It is a small grape, giving very deep color and extract, quite resistant to disease and capable of producing wines of great longevity, elegance and structure. It is grown throughout the winemaking world as both a single varietals and a blending grape, where it imparts a classic quality to many local indigenous varieties. It has been particularly successful in Australia, California and South America where the long, warm ripening season and diverse soils realize the grape's true potentials. It has a natural affinity with oak, which imparts the wonderful cedar and 'cigar box' attributes for which the grape is famous.

2004

Joffré
Valle de Uco,
Mendoza

Polished & elegant, with good berry flavors balanced with green olive, dill, unsweetened chocolate & earth. Feels plush in the mouth, smooth & soft.

50 Recipes & glass of Wine

Baked Manicotti

Ingredients

- 1 package of 16 manicotti shells

- 8 oz. grated Parmesan cheese

- 6 cloves garlic, minced

- 1 16oz. tub of Ricotta cheese

- 8-12 oz. fresh hot Italian bulk sausage

- 1 cup fresh cut parsley

- 3 cans of crushed tomatoes in sauce

- 16 oz. Mozzarella cheese, shredded

DIRECTIONS

Cook the manicotti according to package directions. Be careful not to overcook. In a large nonstick fry pan, thoroughly cook the sausage, breaking it into small bite-sized pieces and drain. In a mixing bowl, whisk together the sausage, ricotta, Parmesan cheese, garlic, pepper & parsley.

Stuff each manicotti shell with the mixture and place in a nonstick baking dish. Pour tomato sauce over the manicotti, and top with the mozzarella cheese and bake for 45 minutes at 350°F.

Chef Recommended Wine

Ciacci Piccolomini d'Aragona
Rosso di Montalcino

Grape Variety

Carignan

Most popular red grape variety grown in the Languedoc-Roussillon region of France. Used as a blend, where it can account for as much as 60% of the cépage, it is late ripening, resistant to spring frosts, tolerant of heat and gives high tannin, extract and color. Now popular in California and South America as well as Northern Spain, where it is known as 'Cariñena'.

2004

Ciacci
Piccolomini
d'Aragona
Rosso di
Montalcino

Brilliant ruby red, vinous,
intense, fruity, sweet spices,
soft, fresh, rightly tannic,
tasty, well-structured,
pleasant toasty note in the
ending.

50 Recipes & glass of Wine

Beet Salad

Ingredients

- 1 pound beets, cooked & sliced
- 3 oranges, peeled & sliced
- 1/3 cup walnuts
- 3 tablespoons orange juice
- 1 teaspoon lemon juice
- 1/4 teaspoon salt
- 3 Tbsp. Extra virgin olive oil
- 2 ounces Parmigiano
- Freshly ground pepper

DIRECTIONS

Pat beets dry. Arrange beets and orange slices in an attractive, overlapping pattern on a large serving platter or on individual plates.

Toast walnuts in a preheated 350° oven until light golden brown, about 10 minutes. Chop finely and sprinkle over the beets and oranges.

Whisk orange juice, lemon juice and salt together in a small bowl. Add oil in a thin, steady stream, whisking constantly. Pour dressing over salad.

Make 1/2 cup of thin slivers of Parmigiano with a vegetable peeler. Scatter over the salad. Season with freshly ground pepper and serve immediately.

Chef Recommended Wine

Planeta Merlot

Grape Variety

Chardonnay

The classic white varietals of Burgundy and perhaps the best known and loved white varietals in the world. It is vigorous, easy to grow but susceptible to spring frosts as witnessed regularly by the vigorous of Chablis. It grows well in cooler climates but can lose acidity if picked late, especially in warmer regions such as Australia and California. Its typical varietals characteristics are honeyed, tropical fruit flavors with toasty, buttery nuances. It ages well and is totally at home with oak, which imparts those delicious vanilla and butterscotch tones so beloved of Burgundy drinkers. Its diversity of style can perhaps account for some of its worldwide appeal.

Chenin Blanc

Classic white varietals of France's Loire Valley and now grown throughout the world. Known for its rather unusual 'wet-wool', 'damp straw' aromas, it tends to be more floral than fruity when young and gives high acidity, growing well in marginal climates. It ages well and its susceptibility to 'botrytis'* produces some of the great sweet wines of the Loire, for example Quarts de Chaume and Vouvray. It is grown widely in South Africa where it is known as 'Steen'.

2003

Planeta Merlot

The color is an intense red with strong ruby hue. The nose is complex, with mineral notes of graphite and fling, alongside the fruit (red berries & plums, blueberry & mulberry). The scent highlights incude hints of balsam & musk, laurel & leather. The palate is not too concentrated, elegant, with lively tannis, refined & spicy with a mint notes on finish.

50 Recipes & glass of Wine

Farfalle with Smoked Salmon & Peas

Ingredients

- 2 Tbsp. olive oil
- 1 medium red onion
- 3 cloves garlic, minced
- 1/4 teaspoon crushed red pepper
- 12 oz. farfalle (bowtie) pasta
- 1 cup frozen peas
- 4 oz. package smoked salmon cut into thin strips
- 1/4 cup fresh dill
- Zest of 1 lemon
- Salt & pepper to taste

Start to finish, 20 minutes

Chef Recommended Wine

Paso Robles
Wite Zinfandel

DIRECTIONS

Bring a large pot of lightly salted water to a boil. While the water heats, combine the olive oil, onion, garlic, & red pepper in a large skillet set over a medium-high heat. Sauté, stirring frequently, until the onions are tender and just translucent, about 6 minutes. Add the pasta to the boiling water and cook until al dente, or just firm at the center, about 8 minutes, or as the packaging directs. While the pasta cooks, add the peas to the onions and cook until peas are heated through. Remove the skillet from the heat. Once the pasta has cooked, use a slotted spoon to transfer it and a bit of water clinging to it to the skillet. If you would rather drain the pasta, first reserve 1/4 cup of the cooking water and add it to the skillet along with the pasta. Add the salmon, dill & lemon zest to the skillet and toss well to combine. The heat of the pasta will mostly cook the salmon, but it need not be cooked through. Season to taste with salt & pepper.

Grape Variety

Cinsaut

Sometimes spelt Cinsault, this red variety is a popular constituent of the wines of Southern France, notably Châteauneuf-du-Pape and the Midi. It is an early ripened, gives intense color and flavor and can withstand very hot climates. It is one of the blending grapes of the South African 'Pinotage' where it is known as 'Hermitage' after the Northern Rhône region - why? nobody knows, as Cinsaut is neither used nor permitted in this region of France.

Dolcetto

Italian red grape from the Piedmont area of the North West. Produces soft varietals wines for early drinking. Gives lots of up front fruit with soft tannins with a style not unlike the Gamay of Beaujolais.

Gamay

The red grape of Beaujolais. Vinified by a process known as 'macération carbonique'* if produces light, fruit driven wines for early consumption. At home in the granite hills of Beaujolais it is a vigorous producer but susceptible to rot. Sometimes blended with Pinot Noir under the appellation 'Bourgogne Passe-Tout-Grains'. Also grown quite extensively in the Loire Valley notably in Touraine.

2005

Paso Robles
Wite
Zinfandel

Maddalena Vineyard White Zinfandel greets the nose with aromas of violets and strawberries. the bright, crisp mouth is sweet with ripe flavors of raspberries and kiwi fruit. The color is brilliant rose with purple hues.

Sautéed Sea Bass
on Bruschetta

Ingredients

- 2 lbs. whole Italian tomatoes cut into 1/2 inch cubes

- 1/4 cup parsley tops, chopped

- 1 tablespoon basil, freshly chopped

- 3 garlic cloves, chopped finely

- 2 teaspoons dry oregano

- 3 Tbsp. fresh lemon juice

- 3 Tbsp. Balsamic vinegar

- 8 to 10 diagonal 1/4 inch thick slices of Italian bread toasted

- 3 tablespoons butter

- 8 @ 6~8 oz. sea bass, flounder, or sole fillets

Chef Recommended Wine

Vernaccia di San Gimignano Panizzi

DIRECTIONS

In a bowl stir together tomatoes, parsley, oregano, garlic, lemon juice, vinegar & salt & pepper to taste. Drain mixture in a sieve set over a bowl for 10 minutes, reserving liquid, to divide among toasts, spreading to cover. Season fish with salt & pepper in a large nonstick skillet. Heat butter over moderately high heat until foam subsides.

Cook fish for 3 minutes on each side, or until just cooked through. Arrange 1 fillet over each Bruschetta and keep warm.

Add reserved tomato liquid in a skillet and boil until reduced to about 1/3 cup. Pour over fish. Serve with your choice of vegetables.

Grape Variety

Gewurztraminer

Difficult to pronounce, the 'gewurzt' means 'spice' in German, it is also one of the easier varietals to recognize because of its distinct perfumed aroma, likened to rose petals and lychees. Best known in the wines of Alsace where it is designated a 'noble' grape and a permitted variety for the Grand Crus. It produces very aromatic wines with up to 14% alcohol and can be an excellent companion to oriental cuisine.

Grenache

Thought to have originated in Spain, where it is known as Garnacha, this is a hot climate red grape ideally suited to the Languedoc region of France and the Navarra region of Spain. It is primarily a blending grape, thin skinned, so giving lighter color. It is often used to add subtlety to the more beefy southern reds. Has become very popular in California and Australia where it can be seen as single varietals.

Lambrusco

Famous for the 'frizzante', semi sweet wines found in 1 liter screw cap bottles; this grape originates near Modena in the Emilia-Romagna region of Central Italy. Much maligned by 'serious' wine drinkers, it produces a fresh, semi sweet, fruit driven wine usually low in alcohol and quite inexpensive. Very popular in the United States.

2005

Vernaccia di San Gimignano Panizzi

Vernaccia is one of Italy's oldest native grapes. This version from a 325 acre vineyard near Tuscany's famed "city of towers" is not aromatically intense but it does offer nice melon and floral tones.
Tart and flinty in the mouth.

Caprese Chicken Salad

Ingredients

- 1 Mozzarella di Bufala Campana
- 4 Cherry tomatoes, cut in quarters
- 1 breast of chicken, grilled or pan-fried
- 2 stems of fresh basil
- Extra virgin olive oil
- Salt to taste

Chef Recommended Wine

Phantom
Bogle

DIRECTIONS

The experts say that Mozzarella di Bufala Campana should be savored freshly made.
If it has been refrigerated, remove it and bring it to room temperature several hours before serving.

Wash & cut the cherry tomatoes. Wash the basil & remove the leaves from the stems. Slice the Mozzarella di Bufala Campana.

Arrange in a plate, a bed of green salad of your choice, cut the cherry tomato, then slice the mozzarella, drizzle the olive oil, sprinkle some salt, garnish with basil leaves.

The Caprese salad made with Mozzarella di Bufala Campana is the most famous & refreshing of all Italian summer dishes. Garnish it with grilled or toasted sliced bread.

Grape Variety

Malbec

This red grape accounted for the famous 'black wine' of Cahors where it is known as the 'Cot' and the 'Auxerrois', and just to confuse matters further, when grown in St. Emilion, it is known as the 'Pressac'. A small, dark, thick-skinned grape, it gives intense color, big tannins and lots of structure to the wines and is generally blended with a little Merlot for subtlety. Has become very popular in Argentina where it adapts well to the hot climate.

2003

Phantom Bogle

Head-trained, dry farmed old vines are again the source for Bogle's Old Vine zinfandel. These gnarly old vines produce concentrated fruit of unsurpassed quality & intensity. This supple and mouth-filling vintage leads with juicy blueberry & ripe blackberry fruit. Black pepper and deep cedar notes integrate well this soft, plush body. Subtle hints of spicy oak & pipe tobacco create structure, allowing this wine to pair with everything from rich sauces & unique dishes to your favorite weeknight take-out.

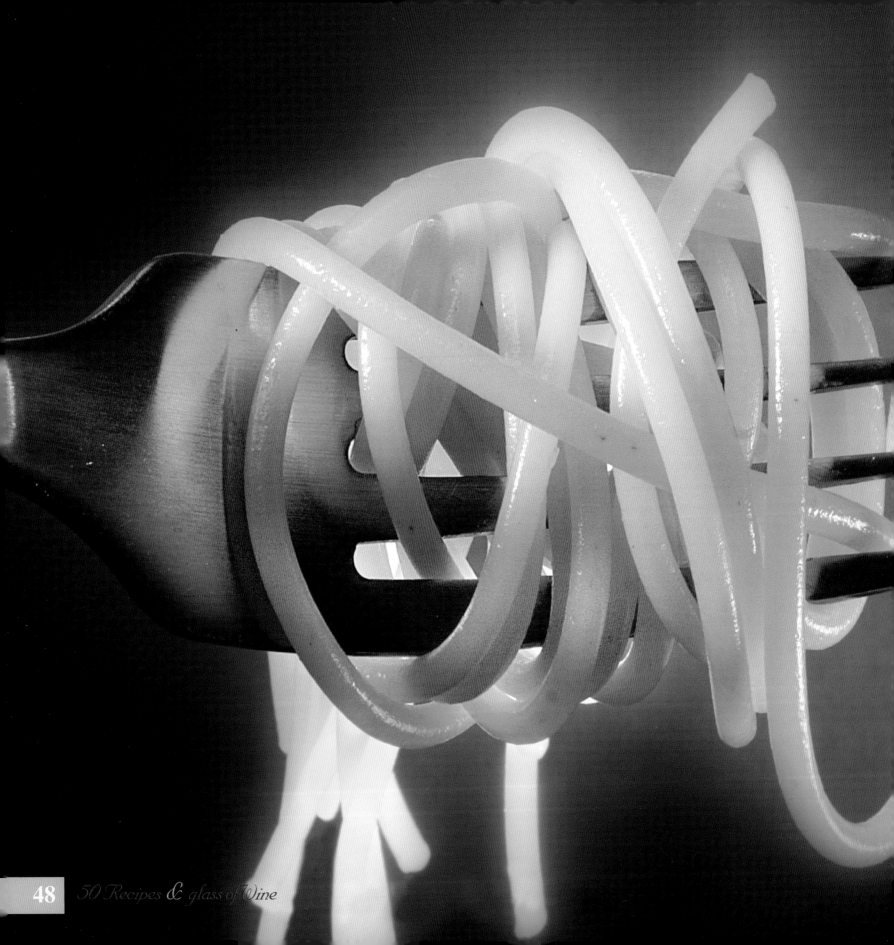

Spaghetti alla Carbonara

Ingredients

- 1 lb. spaghetti
- 4 oz. pancetta
- 2 tbs. olive oil
- 3 egg yolks
- 4 oz. grated Pecorino
- Salt & pepper

DIRECTIONS

Heat olive oil in a skillet over medium-high heat. Add diced pancetta and fry until crisp and brown, for 5-6 minutes. Remove from heat and set aside. In a bowl beat together egg yolks, Pecorino cheese, salt and a generous amount of pepper. Set aside.

Cook the spaghetti in plenty of boiling salted water until al dente; strain and pour back into pot. Over a low flame, add the cooked pancetta and the egg mix, allowing the heat to cook the eggs for a few minutes. Toss well & sprinkle with more cheese.

Serve immediately.

Chef Recommended Wine

Le Volte

Grape Variety

Marsanne

White grape of the Northern Rhône and primary constituent of white Crozes-Hermitage and St.Joseph it is also a permitted blend for red Hermitage. It produces wines high in extract and alcohol with pronounced floral and almond characteristics. Often blended with the more refined Roussanne for a touch of elegance. Seen as varietals in the Victoria region of Australia, notably Chateau Tahbilk.

Merlot

The second 'noble' red grape of Bordeaux and the first in St. Emilion and Pomerol. Responsible for that delicious, plummy, soft style of wine it is an ideal blend with the more austere Cabernet. It is an adaptable grape that ripens early, gives great color and fruit sweetness, but is susceptible to spring frosts and to rot. It has become extremely popular throughout the world in both its blended and varietals form, especially in Italy, Australia and Chile. Its most hallowed 'claim to fame' is perhaps Pomerol's 'Château Pétrus, one of the world's most expensive and sought after wines.

2004

Le Volte

Harmoniously blending three noble grape varities, Le Volte combines the brisk acidity & Tuscan personality of Sangiovese with the rich, plumy flavors of Cabernet Sauvignon & Merlot. It is a seductively fragrant wine of great charm & finesse.

Fettuccine with Chicken in Cream sauce

Ingredients

- 12 ounces Chicken Breast, skinless & boneless
- 1 tablespoon butter
- 1 cup of snap peas
- 1 cup of cherry tomatoes
- 1 small red onion, thinly sliced
- 1/2 teaspoon dried red pepper, crushed
- 1 cup whipping cream
- 2 cloves of garlic, minced
- 1 cup chicken stock
- 3 tablespoons fresh basil, thinly sliced
- 1/4 cup finely grated Parmesan Cheese
- 8 ounces fettuccine
- Additional grated Parmesan Cheese

DIRECTIONS

Sprinkle chicken with salt & pepper. Melt butter in heavy large skillet over medium high heat. Add chicken and cook until brown on both sides, about 5 minutes. Transfer chicken to plate. Add minced garlic, snap peas & cherry tomatoes. Sauté until crisp tender, for 5 minutes. Add whipping cream & chicken stock. Simmer until sauce thickens slightly, for 8 minutes.

Cut chicken into strips & add to sauce. Simmer until chicken is cooked through, about 2 minutes. Add basil and 1/4 cup grated Parmesan cheese to sauce, stirring to incorporate. Season sauce to taste with salt & pepper.

Meanwhile, cook pasta in large pot of boiling water until tender, but still firm to bite. Drain & return to pot. Add sauce & toss to coat.

Chef Recommended Wine

Provenance Rutherford Cabernet

Grape Variety

Muscat

There is no single Muscat grape but rather a family of grapes - over 200 in total - to which the name Muscat is appended. They are generally associated with aromatic, full flavored wines with distinct floral and musky tones. They can be vinified dry, as in Alsace, sweet as in the Italian 'Moscato' and fortified as in Muscat Beaumes-de-Venise etc. In Spain the variety is known as 'Moscatel', in South Africa 'Muskadel' and many wine lovers have enjoyed the sumptuous delights of the Liqueur 'Brown' Muscats of Australia.

Nebbiolo

The red grape of Barolo and Barbaresco from the Piedmont region of Northwest Italy. Named after the word 'nebbia', or fog in Italian, which rises around the hills of Alba, the famous truffle countryside. It is noted for its high acidity and 'mouth puckering' tannins and its distinct bouquet of black cherries, liquorices and leather. A top Barolo will take years to soften but when mature will evolve the vegetal, gamy characteristics for which this Italian classic is famous. The color on ageing Nebbiolo wines fades rapidly to form a distinctive brownish rim.

2003

Provenance Rutherford Cabernet

Initially closed in showing mescal, minerality & beeswax, this wine opens to mocha, soy, French vanilla ice cream with chocolate nuances, & the classic cocoadust finish. This is a bordelaise-style wine in its depth & its "hidden treasure" fruit elegance & subtely. It is surprisingly soft & approachable with sweet oak spice & black olive throughout the finish.

Chicken Gumbo Soup

Ingredients

- 8 cups of water
- 1 teaspoon garlic powder
- 1 tablespoon hot pepper sauce
- 2 carrots, sliced thin
- 4 ounces fresh mushrooms
- 1 (10 oz.) package frozen okra
- 1/4 cup uncooked wild rice
- 1 chicken breast, skinless & boneless cut into cubes
- 1-1/2 cups uncooked rice
- Salt & freshly ground pepper to taste
- 3 green onions, thinly sliced

DIRECTIONS

Bring the water to boil. Add the garlic powder and the hot pepper sauce.

Put the carrots and mushrooms into the pot of water.
Cook for five minutes.

Add the okra, wild rice and chicken cubes.

Turn heat to low, and cook for three hours. Add salt and pepper to taste.

Serve hot, garnished with green onions.

**Chef
Recommended
Wine**

Aristos

2004

Aristos

Brillant garnet-ruby red hue. Cherry, sage, dried herb & earth aromas.
Medium-full bodied with very good concentration, this wine has firm tannins and moderate acidity along with an earthy, slightly peppery finish.

Citrus Salad

Ingredients

- 1/4 cup olive oil
- 2 tablespoons sugar
- 1 tsp. finely shredded lemon peel
- 1 tablespoons lemon juice
- 1/4 teaspoon salt
- 3 large oranges, peeled and sectioned
- 1 large pink grapefruit, peeled & sectioned
- 1 medium red onion, sliced (2 Tbsp.)
- 1 tablespoons snipped fresh mint
- 4 cups Spring Mix (about 6 oz.)

DIRECTIONS

For dressing, in a screw-top jar combine oil, sugar, lemon peel, lemon juice, & salt.
Cover and shake well.

In a medium bowl place orange and grapefruit sections, onion, and mint. Pour dressing over and toss gently. Cover and refrigerate 2 to 24 hours.

To serve, put Spring Mix in a large salad bowl and top with fruit mixture; toss lightly. Serve Immediately.

Chef Recommended Wine

Curvee Du Golfe De St. Tropez

Grape Variety

Pinotage

South Africa's famous red wine is in fact a man made strain, created in 1925 by crossing Pinot Noir with Cinsaut (known locally as Hermitage). It had received some bad press for its quality levels but in recent years has produced some stunning wines from the top growers, with huge fruit concentration and ageing potential. Be prepared to pay for the quality but it's worth it.

Pinot Blanc

Known as Pinot Bianco in Italy and Weissburgunder in Germany this white grape produces fresh varietals wines with apple and citrus aromas for early drinking. It performs well in cooler climates with medium to high yields and good sugar levels.

Pinot Gris

Known as Pinot Grigio in Italy and Rulander in Germany it is believed to have mutated from the Pinot Noir. Widely grown throughout Europe but particularly in Alsace and northern Italy it produces relatively full- bodied wines with a slight yeasty aroma. It is highly thought of in Alsace where it is known as Tokay d'Alsace or Tokay Pinot Gris and is permitted for Grand Cru wines. Here it is also used to produce the luscious 'vendange tardive' or late harvested sweet wines.

2005

Curvee Du Golfe De St. Tropez

Rose de Provence. A full flavor, light body & refreshing dry rose from Grenache.

Linguine with Clam Sauce

Ingredients

- 1/4 cup extra virgin olive oil
- 1/4 teaspoon red pepper flakes
- 12 oz. whole baby clams
- 16 oz. minced clams
- 2 garlic cloves, minced
- 1/4 teaspoon salt
- 1/3 cup dry white wine
- 3 tablespoons parsley, chopped

DIRECTIONS

Drain and reserve juice in the cans of minced and whole baby clams. In a medium saucepan, heat oil.

Add garlic and sauté for 2 minutes. Add reserved clam juices, wine, red pepper flakes and salt.
Bring to boil and simmer for 10 minutes.

Add all clams and parsley. Return to boil, then keep warm while preparing linguine. When linguine is done, pour white clam sauce over top and toss gently and serve.

Sprinkle more parsley.
Makes enough for 6 servings.

Chef Recommended Wine

Argiolas
Vermentino di Sardegna
Costamolino

Grape Variety

Pinot Noir

The classic red grape of Burgundy and responsible for some of the world's most expensive and sought after wines. Packed full of juicy strawberry fruits when young, at its top level it matures into a complex masterpiece with vegetal and farmyard tones. It is, however, a poor traveller and difficult to cultivate in hot climates. Purists will argue that its home is Burgundy and that is where it should remain - doubtless producers in Oregon and Carneros will differ. Pinot is however capable of producing very mediocre wine, at worst thin and acidic, and many people buying at the lower Burgundian levels have been disappointed. Good Pinots are available and worth seeking out, the best are sublime but sadly, out of reach for the average pocket.

Riesling

Germany's 'noble' white grape and revered the world over. It produces a diversity of wine styles from sweet to dry, from fresh and youthful to mature and mellow - Riesling has enormous ageing potential and takes on the character of the various regions in which it is planted. It is a grower's dream in view of its versatility and can flourish from the cool slopes of Germany's Saar region to the warm valleys of California. It is responsible for the luscious and rare Beerenauslesen and Trockenbeerenauslen (T.B.A) which retain freshness, high acidity but low alcohol and intense fruit ripeness. A true aristocrat of a grape.

2005

Argiolas Vermentino di Sardegna Costamolino

Deceptively graceful at first, with a Burgundian-like perfume, this quickly delivers a torrent of fruit-blackberry, boysenberry & black currant, that cascades over itself, pushed from behind by flavors of mocha, mineral, tar & violets. Long, sweet & pure through a densely structured finish.

French Onion Soup

Ingredients

- 1/4 cup butter
- 3 onions, thinly sliced
- 1 teaspoon white sugar
- 1 Tbsp. All-purpose flour
- 2 - 1/2 cups water
- 1/2 cup red wine
- 2 (10.5 oz.) cans beef broth
- 1 French baguette
- 8 oz. Swiss cheese

Chef Recommended Wine

Sonoma Coast
Pinot Noir

DIRECTIONS

Melt butter in a 4 quart saucepan. Stir in sugar. Cook onions over medium heat for 10 minutes, or until golden brown.

Stir in flour until well blended with the onions and pan juices. Add water, wine, and beef broth; heat to boiling. Reduce heat to low. Cover soup, and simmer for 10 minutes.

Cut four 1 inch slices of bread from the baguette. Toast the bread slices at 325° just until browned, about 10 minutes.

Reserve the remaining bread to serve with soup. Ladle soup into 4 12 oz., oven-safe bowls. Place 1 slice toasted bread on top of soup in each bowl. Fold Swiss cheese slices, and fit on toasted bread slices. Place bowls on cookie sheet for easier handling. Bake at 425° for 10 minutes, or just until cheese melts.

Grape Variety

Sangiovese

The red grape of Tuscany and notably, Chianti and Brunello di Montalcino, it is second only to Barbera as Italy's most planted red variety. It is a thin skinned grape that gives medium body but high acidity. Cherry like when young, it develops into a mature wine with black cherry and liquorices aromas. It blends very well with Cabernet Sauvignon as witnessed in the great Tuscan 'Vini da Tavolas' but has not proved too popular outside Italy. Some plantings are found in California, Australia and Argentina but its home is very much in the Tuscan hills.

Sauvignon Blanc

Synonymous with fresh gooseberry and green apple aromas in its varietals form, Sauvignon Blanc is one of the most traveled white grapes in the world. Its home is certainly France where it bends with the 'fatter' Semillon to make white Bordeaux wines from the dry Graves style to the luscious botrytised* Sauternes. In the Loire it is responsible for such famous marques as Sancerre and Pouilly-Fumé where it is found in its purest form. The New World has adopted the grape with great acclaim (and success), notably New Zealand, Argentina and Chile where its crisp fresh acidity and citrus fruit character are to the fore. As a dry wine it is best-drunk young and fresh.

2003

*Sonoma Coast
Pinot Noir*

Monstruous amounts of intense cherry liqueurish fruit dominate the nose with a warm blush of French Oak and spicy blackberry juice undertones. The palate again bursts with intense fruit & a dusty Asian spice, intense & viscous.

50 Recipes & glass of Wine

Fusilli Pasta &
Black Bean Salad

DIRECTIONS

Rinse beans. Dehydrate beans by soaking them overnight; or cover with water, bring to a boil, then turn off the heat and let them sit for an hour. Drain and rinse. In large stockpot, sauté onion, pepper, celery & parsley in olive oil for 5 minutes.

After sauté mixture, add drained beans, spices, chicken stock; then bring to a boil. Reduce heat.

Simmer until beans are tender, about 2 hours, stirring gently every 20-30 minutes. When beans are done to your liking, add salt to taste. Boil fusilli pasta al dente.

Cool pasta with cold water. In a large bowl, mix all together. Keep in refrigerator for 1 hour and serve with sprinkle of grated cheese.

Ingredients

- 1 lb. dried black beans
- 2 tablespoons olive oil
- 1 medium onion, chopped
- 1 chopped red, yellow, & green bell pepper
- 5 cloves of garlic
- 1-1/2 Tbsp. ground & dried red chiles
- 1 cup of 1/2 parsley & 1/2 celery, chopped
- 1/2 teaspoon ground allspice
- 6 cups of chicken stock

Chef Recommended Wine

Argiano
Brunello di Montalcino

Grape Variety

Sémillon

A thin skinned grape producing wines of high extract and flavor but soft acidity. In France it combines with Sauvignon Blanc to make the white wines of Bordeaux, most notably the sweet dessert wines of Sauternes and Barsac. Its thin skin leaves it susceptible to the fungus botrytis* the much sought after 'noble rot' in these sweet wine regions. As varietals it has fared best in Australia, notably the Hunter Valley, where it produces well-rounded wines with lots of tropical fruits and honeyed tones. Here too it is blended with Chardonnay and oak aged to give an added dimension.

2001

Argiano
Brunello di
Montalcino

Full red. Highly complex aromas of medicinal black cherry, mocha, licorice & black olive, with a roasted aspect & a whiff of celery seed. Sweet, densely packed and concentrated, with lush, seamless dark fruit flavors spreading out to saturate the palate. A big, firmly structured Brunello that finishes with ripe tannins & intriguing hints of iron & peat.

50 Recipes & glass of Wine

Grilled Garlic Shrimp

Ingredients

- 2 pounds jumbo shrimps, shelled & deveined, tail on
- 1 large clove of garlic
- Salt
- Juice of 1 lemon
- 2-3 tablespoons
- 1/4 cup olive oil
- Garlic butter recipe

Garlic Sauce

- 1/2 cup butter
- 1 teaspoon Worcestershire sauce
- 1 tablespoon lemon juice
- Dash or two hot pepper sauce
- 1 large clove garlic, crushed
- Salt

DIRECTIONS

Use scissors to remove shells without disturbing tails. In a glass bowl or food storage bag, combine garlic, salt, lemon juice, and olive oil.

Put shrimp in bowl; stir to coat well. Cover and refrigerate for 2 hours.

Thread marinated shrimp onto skewers & grill 5 to 6 inches from coals for about 12 to 15 minutes, turning frequently. If broiling, remove tails.

Serve shrimp with garlic butter, for dipping.

To make garlic sauce, melt butter; add remaining ingredients. Heat through and serve with the grilled shrimp or other seafood.

Chef Recommended Wine

Sancerre
White

Grape Variety

Syrah (or Shiraz)

The classic red grape of the northern Rhône where it produces such wines as Hermitage, Côte Rôtie, Crozes Hermitage and St. Joseph to name but a few. It produces intense inky purple colored wines when young with a distinctly spicy tone. As it matures it turns to deep garnet with evolving earthy, stewed blackberry and damson flavors. It gives huge extract and tannins and is capable of great ageing. As 'Shiraz' in Australia it presents a more approachable nature, more plummy and elegant when young but still retaining that spicy character and intense color. Often blended in the New World with Cabernet Sauvignon for added complexity. It is best suited to hot climates and granite soils.

Tempranillo

The Tempranillo is to Rioja what Pinot Noir is to Burgundy. By far Spain's most noble indigenous grape it has similar characteristics to the Pinot - strawberries when young, earthy vegetal when mature - and it ages very well. It ripens early ('temprana' is the Spanish for 'early') is thick-skinned and gives good color and extract but low alcohol and acidity. In Rioja it is blended with the more fiery Garnacha and a little Mazuelo and Graciano. It is grown throughout Spain but very much as a grape for blending as opposed to straight varietals. Outside Spain the grape is quite prolific in Argentina and to a lesser extent in California.

2005

Sancerre White

White Sancerre comes from the sauvignon Blanc grape. This makes a semi-dry fresh, fruity white wine with vegetable flavors.

50 Recipes & glass of Wine

Grilled Fish Steaks

Ingredients

- 4 (6 oz.) dense fish steaks, such as Halibut, swordfish or tuna
- 1/2 cup vegetable oil
- 3 tablespoons soy sauce
- 2 tablespoons medium dry sherry
- 1-1/2 tsp. ginger root, peeled & grated
- 1 tsp. fresh grated orange rind
- Fresh ground pepper to taste
- Oil as needed for the grill

Chef Recommended Wine

Champalou
Vouvray

DIRECTIONS

Garnish as desired: Fresh scallions, red onion over wild rice.

Arrange the steaks in a shallow glass or porcelain baking dish. Whisk the rest of the ingredients until creamy and emulsified. Pour the marinade over the fish.

Marinate, covered, 2 hours or overnight turning periodically. Heat a ridged grill until hot.

Brush with additional oil and heat the oil. Grill the steaks over high heat on both sides according
to thickness (about 10 minutes).

You may also grill the fish over charcoal.

Garnish and serve. This is really easy and tastes great!

Grape Variety

Viognier

A relatively obscure vine, difficult to grow and cultivate and capable of only tiny yields, Viognier owes its reputation to the fine wines it produces in the northern Rhône, namely Condrieu and Château Grillet. It has a distinct orange blossom and apricot aroma together with a golden yellow color, huge weight of tropical fruits with a broad weighty structure and quite high in alcohol. It is produced to a lesser extent as a Vin de Pays in the Languedoc and there are also some plantings in California. Its low yields and associated difficulties are unlikely to elevate it to the commercial status. Worth seeking out though!

Zinfandel

Known simply as 'Zin', this is California's most common red wine grape. It produces all styles of wine - red, white and rosé from bone dry to sweet, even a port style from late harvested grapes. For years it was dismissed as a quaffing jug wine not to be taken seriously. Things have changed, however, and we are now seeing some pretty serious offerings coming from the better producers. It is rarely blended and is at its best as a dry red wine with aromas of ripe strawberry fruits and a whiff of spice. It prefers cooler climates, as it can tend to over ripen.

2004

Champalou Vouvray

Minerality, wet wool and citrus notes meld into a beautiful bouquet backed by a line of acidity that carries the wine. Enjoy with tuna nicoise, shellfish or cheese or well-chilled on a warm day.

84 Recipes & glass of Wine

Grilled Salmon & Cucumber

Ingredients

- 1/3 cup fresh lemon juice
- 1/3 cup extra virgin olive oil
- 1/3 cup shallots, chopped
- 1 tablespoon lemon peel, grated
- 1 medium fresh cucumber, peeled, sliced fine
- 2 tablespoons fresh parsley, chopped
- Nonstick vegetable oil spray
- (1) 3 pound salmon fillet

DIRECTIONS

Whisk first 6 ingredients in small bowl. Season marinade with salt & pepper.

Combine 1/2 cup marinade, cucumber in medium bowl, let stand 30 minutes; toss occasionally.

Spray barbecue rack with non-stick spray and prepare barbecue (medium high heat). Place salmon on the grill and brush with marinade sauce. Let cook 5 minutes on each side.

Take the slices of marinated cucumber and put in center of the plate.

Lay the grilled salmon on the cucumber salad.

Chef Recommended Wine

Catena Chardonnay

50 Recipes & glass of Wine

2004

Catena Chardonnay

Full yellow-gold. Rather exotic aromas of apricot, orange, honey and smokey oak. Then sweet but firm, with very intense flavors of apricot, peach, kiwi and minerals (Catena described these flavors as "acidic tropical fruits") Catenas' chardonnays are consistently among the elite of Argentina, as few other producers manage to capture this much freshness of fruit.

Baked Haddock with Tarragon Marinade

Ingredients

- 2 Tbsp. rice or white wine vinegar
- 2 Tbsp. olive oil
- 2 Tbsp. Dijon Mustard
- 1/2 Tbsp. chopped fresh tarragon leaves
- 1/8 teaspoon pepper
- 1 to 11/2 lbs. haddock fillets

DIRECTIONS

In a large bowl whisk the vinegar, oil, mustard, tarragon & pepper.

Rinse the fish and pat dry. Add the fish to the marinade and turn the pieces to coat completely. Let marinate 15 minutes. Lay the fish, overlapping thin areas, in a shallow baking pan and drizzle with any remaining marinade. Bake, uncovered, in a 450°F oven until fish flakes in the thickest part when prodded with a fork and flesh is opaque, about 7 minutes for fish 3/4 inch thick.

Serve on a bed of vegetables & garnish with a sundried tomato.

Chef Recommended Wine

Nobilo
Sauvignon Blanc

Earth and Spice

Caramelized
Butterscotch - Riesling, California Chardonnay
Caramel - Extensively oak-aged wines, Port
Chocolate - Cabernet Sauvignon, Shiraz, other oak-aged reds, mature reds
Honey - Sauternes, Riesling, Viognier
Molasses - Sherry, fortified wines
Soy Sauce - Sake, some sparkling wines

Chemical
Bubblegum - Beaujolais Nouveau, Pinotage, some rosé, cool-fermented whites
Candle Wax (Lanolin) - Sémillon
Cold cream - Gewürztraminer
Gasoline/Petrol - Mature German and Austrian Riesling
Perfume - Many wines, especially whites
Tar - Barolo, northern Rhône wines

Earth
Flint - Chablis, Pouilly-Fumé, Sancerre
Mineral - Pouilly-Fumé, Riesling, Chablis
Stone/gravel - Graves, other rustic reds
Salt - Sherry, particularly Manzanilla
Wet stones - Chablis

Nutty
Almond/Marzipan - Soave, Prosecco, some Burgundies, Valpolicella
Chestnut - Southern Italian wines
Hazelnut - New World Chardonnay, Champagne
Nut - Mature Champagne, white Burgundy, other Chardonnay, other oak-aged wines

2005

Nobilo
Sauvignon Blanc

Tart style is like a mouthful of lime juise with just enough apple and pear flavors to round it out. Finishes savory and refreshing.

Broiled Chicken Kabobs

Ingredients

- Chicken Breasts (about 2 lbs.)
- 1/4 cup of soy sauce
- 1 tablespoons vegetable oil
- 1 teaspoon packed brown sugar
- 1/4 teaspoon ground ginger
- 1 clove garlic, crushed
- Diced fresh apples

DIRECTIONS

Remove bones and skin from chicken breasts. Cut chicken into 3/4 inch pieces. Mix chicken, soy sauce, oil, brown sugar, ginger and garlic in glass bowl. Cover and refrigerate, stirring occasionally, at least 2 hours.

Remove chicken from marinade, thread 4 or 5 chicken pieces onto bamboo skewer. Cut apples in large squares and alternate apples with chicken on each bamboo skewer.

Brush chicken with reserved marinade. Set oven control to broil or 550 •. Broil skewers with tops about 4 inches from heat for 4 to 5 minutes; turn. Brush with marinade. Broil until chicken is done, 4 to 5 minutes longer.

Chef Recommended Wine

Tommasi
Amarone

Earth and Spice

Spice
Black Pepper - Syrah, some Grenache-based wines
Cinnamon - Rhone reds, oak-aged whites
Clove - Cabernet Sauvignon, new oak-aged wines, Gewürztraminer

Gingerbread - Mature Alsace Gewürztraminer
Licorice/Anise - Barbera
Mint - New World Cabernet Sauvignon (Napa), Shiraz (Coonawarra)
Nutmeg - Cabernet Sauvignon
Spice - Many reds including Syrah, Shiraz, Zinfandel; Gewürztraminer
Tobacco (cigar box, pipe tobacco) - many reds including Italian and Bordeaux
White Pepper - Grenache, Grüner Veltliner

Wood
Cedar/cigar box - Bordeaux, other good cabs
Vanilla - wines aged in new American oak
Sawdust

2000

Tommasi
Amarone

A full-bodied, corpulent Amarone, this doesn't have a great deal of grace just yet. Instead, its bold flavors of cinnamon and clove, cherry and plum plow ahead ruggedly, finishing long and tannic. This has all the right stuff, it just needs time to settle down.

50 Recipes & glass of Wine

Lamb Chop Dinner

Ingredients

- 10-12 loin lamb chops, about 1 1/2 inches thick
- 1/2 cup olive oil
- 3/4 cup red wine vinegar
- 1 tablespoon dried rosemary
- 2 cloves garlic, minced
- 1/2 teaspoon salt
- 1/4 teaspoon black pepper

DIRECTIONS

Combine all ingredients, except lamb, in a large glass bowl. Place chops in bowl and turn repeatedly to coat well. Cover and refrigerate for 4 to 12 hours. Once marinated, remove chops from fridge and allow to come to room temperature.

Preheat grill for medium-high heat.

Remove chops from marinade and place on a lightly oiled grill rack.

Cook for 8 minutes on each side.

Remove from heat; allow resting for 3-5 minutes, and serving.

Chef Recommended Wine

Tignanello
Antinori

Fauna

Animal
Cat's Pee - Müller-Thurgau, French Sauvignon Blanc
Farmyard/Barnyard/Manure - Great Pinot Noir (subjective), southern French wines
Foxy - "Grapey" flavors found in native American (vitis labrusca) grape varieties
Game - Tempranillo, especially Ribera del Duero; Burgundy; Rhône Valley wines
Leather - Robust wines, Syrah, port

Lactic
Butter - A sign of malolactic fermentation, especially evident in Chardonnay
Cream (or creamy texture) - Good Champagne, Chardonnay
Sweaty - Sauvignon Blanc

Yeasty/Bready
Biscuity - Champagne
Bread - Champagne and other sparkling wine, sur lie whites
Gingerbread - Mature Alsace Gewürztraminer

2001

Tignanello
Antinori

Tignanello is a blend of Sangiovese (80%), Cabernet Sauvignon (15%) & Cabernet Franc (5%) grown in the vineyard of the same name on the Santa Cristina estate located in the Chianti Classico region. After approximately 2 years of aging in "barriques" of 225 liters, the wine is then bottle aged for another year. Tignanello is a rich & spicy wine with hints of smokey wood. Fullbodied, with silky tannins & a medium finish.

50 Recipes & glass of Wine

Braised Lamb Shank

DIRECTIONS

The Lamb Shank Braise: Preheat oven to 315 • F. Trim excess fat from shank; heat cast iron pan. Add 1 tbsp. oil, season shank assertively with salt & pepper, & slowly brown all sides over medium high heat. Remove from pan, discarding excess oil.

Add onion. Cook for 5 minutes. Add carrots, celery, garlic, & bay leaf. Cook until vegetables are caramelized & tender. Add wine & reduce. Add chicken stock & bring to a simmer.

Place shank in deep pan or dish. Pour vegetables & broth over shanks. Bring back to a simmer over medium heat. Cover & braise for about 1 hour 45 minutes or until meat is tender. Remove to cool. Strain vegetables from braising liquid. Simmer liquid to skim all that rises to the top and reduce by half.

Cover
beans with stock & water. Add bay leaf & vegetables, bringing to a simmer.

Season to taste, continuing to simmer until beans are tender, about 45 minutes. Add more water as necessary.

Ingredients

....

- 2 Lamb shanks, preferably hind shanks

- 2 tablespoons Extra Virgin Olive Oil

- Salt & freshly ground pepper

- 1 Spanish yellow onion

- 1 carrot

- 3 garlic cloves

- 1 bay leaf

- 1/2 cup Cabernet Sauvignon

- 1 cup chicken stock

- 1/2 cup Cannellini beans

....

Chef Recommended Wine

Far Niente
Cabernet Sauvignon

Flora

Canned/Cooked Vegetables
Asparagus - Overripe Sauvignon Blanc
Olive - Cabernet Sauvignon
Mushroom - Pinot Meunier in fine Champagne, red Burgundy
Green Beans

Dried Vegetative
Hay - Sauvignon Blanc
Herbs - Sauvignon Blanc
Straw - Sauvignon Blanc, Sancerre

Fresh Vegetables
Cabbage/Cauliflower - Chardonnay, mature Burgundy
Cut Grass - Early picked Sauvignon Blanc, Grüner Veltliner, Sémillon
Currant Leaf - Sauvignon Blanc
Green Pepper - Cabernet Franc, high yielding Cabernet Sauvignon
Eucalyptus - Australian Shiraz and Cabernet Sauvignon

Flowers
Elderflower - Aromatic grape varieties, Sauvignon Blanc
Floral, or flowery - Riesling, Albariño, Viognier, and many other aromatic wines
Geranium - Over-aged Asti, a fault in sweet wine

Honeysuckle
Lavender - Australian wines, Riesling, Muscat, vinho verde, sparkling wines
Rose - Muscat, rosé Champagne
Violet - Finish on Cabernet-based wines, Bordeaux (Graves)

2003

Far Niente Cabernet Sauvignon

The 2003 Far Niente Cabernet Sauvignon has forward aromas of cassis, licorice, anise & tobacco, complemented by notes of black currant, are present on the nose. The plush, silky entry provides an opening to flavors of blackberry & black cherry fruit on the palate, with a dense core of chewy tannin. The fruit darkens on the palate, & notes of toasty oak with an underlying layer of black cherry emerge on the long, sweet finish.

50 Recipes & glass of Wine

Linguine with Lobster Sauce

Ingredients

- 4 lobster tails
- 6 tablespoons olive oil
- 1/3 cup garlic, chopped
- 2 cups diced onion
- 2 cans crushed tomatoes
- 1-1/2 teaspoons dry basil
- 1-1/2 teaspoons oregano
- 1/4 teaspoon salt
- 1/4 to1/2 teaspoon black pepper
- 1 bay leaf
- 2 lbs. linguine
- 1/4 cup heavy cream
- 1/2 cup chopped parsley

Chef Recommended Wine

L.A. Cetto
Cabernet Sauvignon

DIRECTIONS

Remove meat from lobster shells and cut into 1/2 inch pieces. Heat 3 tablespoons oil in a grill pan. Add 3 Tbsp. garlic; sauté 2 minutes. Add lobster meat; sauté 5 minutes. Remove lobster to a bowl; keep covered. Add remaining oil, remaining garlic & onion to skillet and sauté 10 minutes. Add tomatoes, oregano, salt, black pepper, bay leaf and cook over medium-high heat for 15 minutes.

Remove bay leaf and discard. Meanwhile, cook linguine in a large pot of lightly salted boiling water until al dente, firm but tender. Drain and keep warm. Remove 2 cups of tomato mixture to a blender or food processor. Whirl until pureed.

Return pureed mixture to pot. Add lobster meat with any accumulated juices; cook 2 minutes or until lobster is cooked through. Remove from heat. Stir in cream. Place hot pasta in a large serving bowl. Pour sauce over top; top with parsley and toss to mix. Garnish with fresh cherry tomatoes.

Fruits

Berry
Black Cherry - Cabernet or Syrah
Blackberry - Cahors, Madiran, Malbec, Zinfandel, mourvédre
Blackcurrant/Cassis - Cabernet Sauvignon, Claret/meritage, Cabernet Franc, Merlot, Syrah
Cherry, tart - Cool climate Pinot Noir, Barbera
Cranberry - Côte de Beaune reds, Beaujolais
Grape - Cheap German wines, Muscat
Raspberry - Pinot Noir, Gamay, Grenache
Strawberry - Warm climate Pinot Noir, Burgundy, Beaujolais, Rioja, Loire Cabernet

Citrus
Lemon/lime - many whites, Australian Sémillon and Riesling, German Riesling
Grapefruit - Gewürztraminer, New Zealand Sauvignon Blanc, Jurançon Sec
Gooseberry - Sauvignon Blanc
Orange - Many sweet or fortified wines

Dried/Cooked
Dried Fruit - Amarone, sweet and fortified wines
Raisin - Sweet and fortified wines
Other Dried or Cooked Fruits - Baked cherry, baked blackberry, baked raspberry, jam, prunes
baked apple, baked pear, candied fruits

2003

L.A. Cetto Cabernet Sauvignon

This wine has reaqlly ripe blackberry and cherry flavors, soft tannins, a nice fat mouth feel and hints of darker roasted stuff.
Big, smooth & lush, it gathers power & finishes with a big swoop of meaty, fruity, fat flavor.

50 Recipes & glass of Wine

Lobster Salad

Ingredients

- 12 oz. Lobster Meat
- 1 cup mayonnaise
- 1/2 cup celery chopped
- 1 tsp. Balsamic vinegar
- 1 Tbsp. Dijon Mustard
- 1 cup fresh orange peel
- 2 Tbsp. fresh basil, chopped
- 3 Tbsp. fresh parsley, chopped
- Salt & pepper to taste

DIRECTIONS

In a medium mixing bowl, mix all ingredients except lobster meat and parsley until well blended.

Fold in lobster meat and sprinkle with parsley before serving.

Chef Recommended Wine

Claudius
Merlot

Fruits

Tree Fruit
Apple - Many whites. Chardonnay from cooler climates, lighter wines, German Riesling
Apricot - Aromatic wines including Viognier and Riesling, Loire whites; botrytized
            sweet wines (often dried apricot) like Bonnezeaux and Sauternes
Peach - Viognier, Riesling, Muscat, ripe Sauvignon Blanc, botrytized wines
Pear - many whites, especially young and light bodied, a sign of carbonic maceration

Tropical
Banana - Young Alsace Gewürztraminer, inexpensive, and/or New World wines
Coconut - Good old Champagne, New World Chardonnay
Lychee - Gewürztraminer
Pineapple - Ripe New World Chardonnay, Chenin Blanc, botrytized wines

Other Fruits
Fig - Characteristic of potential complexity in young Chardonnay
Jam - New World Merlot, Syrah
Melon - New World Chardonnay, dry rosé wines
Tomato - Sylvaner, Cabernet Sauvignon
Pomegranate - New World Syrah
Quince - Chenin Blanc

2003

Claudius
Merlot

Ripe and fruity in upfront blackberries, currants & oak, with a hint of cocoa, this wine also shows firm tannins. It's young and finishes with that raw quality of a juvenile Cab. Fine now with rich fare.

50 Recipes & glass of Wine

Pappardelle with Wild Mushrooms

Ingredients

- 7 oz pappardelle
- 1/2 lb. shiitake mushrooms
- 1/2 lb.oyster mushrooms
- 1/2 lb. regular white mushrooms
- 1/2 lb. Chanterelle mushrooms or dried porcini mushrooms soaked in warm water for 20 minutes & reserve the soak water
- 1 medium leek
- 4 Tbsp. extra virgin olive oil
- 5 or 6 cloves of garlic, minced
- 2 small shallots, minced
- 1/2 cup Marsala wine (or medium dry sherry)
- 1/2 cup cream
- 1 tbsp. each fresh thyme, tarragon, rosemary & sage
- Freshly grated Asiago cheese

DIRECTIONS

Cook the pappardelle in a large pot of boiling salted water; set aside.

Cut the mushrooms and leek in 1/2 slices. For best effect, cut the leek diagonally.

Heat the oil in a large saucepan and sauté for four 4 to 5 minutes.
Add the Marsala (and if you used the porcini mushrooms, add 2 tbsp. of the reserved soak liquid).

Cook for 3 minutes, then add cream and fresh herbs. Reduce sauce by half. Add pasta and mix thoroughly.

Garnish with Asiago cheese & serve immediately.

Chef Recommended Wine

Marquis Philips Shiraz 9
McLaren Vale

Wine and Food Pairing Tips: Three Easy Steps

1. Drink what you like. Always a great place to start. If you are fond of full-bodied California Chardonnay or lighter wines from Beaujolais, consider drinking it with your meal. Throw out the wine and food rulebook and drink what you like. I have found pleasure in drinking most any wine that I am fond of with good food and good company.

2. Match the weight of the food to the weight of the wine. A simple concept, lighter foods tend to pair well with lighter wines. A light fish dish, or a simple salad paired with a light crisp white such as Pinot Grigio or Muscadet usually works well. Conversely, full-bodied dishes such as veal stew or a New York Strip steak work well with richer wines such as Zinfandel and Cabernet Sauvignon.

3. Be adventurous! We often enjoy the wine experience because it gives us the opportunity to explore new flavors and tastes. The same can be true when selecting a wine to go with your meal. Go wild! Go crazy! If you've never tasted a wine from Rioja, a Pinot Gris from Alsace, or a Pinotage from South Africa Try it…

2004

*Marquis Philips
Shiraz 9
McLaren Vale*

Deep ruby. Explosive aromas of dark cherry preserves, plum, blackberry, smoked meat, espresso & baking spice. Dense, sweet, with vibrant, powerful dark berry flavors & a creamy, lush texture. Finishes with very persistent, sweet boysenberry, and spice notes of cinnamon and mace. A serious but seductive suave wine.

50 Recipes & glass of Wine

Pasta Al Pesto

Ingredients

- 1 cup hot water
- 2 Chicken Bouillon cubes
- 1 (16 ounce) fresh broccoli
- 1/2 cup grated Romano or Parmesan cheese
- 1/4 cup fresh basil leaves
- 2 tablespoons olive oil
- 1 large clove of garlic, peeled
- 1 (9 ounce) Angel Hair Pasta

DIRECTIONS

Combine water and bouillon in small bowl; stir to dissolve.

Place broccoli, broth, cheese, basil, oil, and garlic in food blender; cover. Process until smooth.

Prepare pasta according to package directions.
Toss broccoli pesto with pasta. Season with coarsely ground black pepper.

Chef Recommended Wine

Bishop's Peak

Choosing Wine Glasses

There really is no right or wrong glass for wine tasting or for drinking wine for that matter. However, there are some glasses that are better than others for evaluating wines. First of all, I like to suggest using glasses that you are comfortable using, there are really only two things to remember when considering a wine tasting glass: the size of the glass and the overall shape of the glass.

The more universally used tasting glass is called a chimney shape. Broader on the bottom of the bowl, it tapers upward to a smaller opening. The broader bottom will enable you to hold enough wine and give you plenty of room to swirl the wine, while the smaller opening at the top will help to trap and focus the aromas, allowing you enough of a scent to assess the wine.

2003

Bishop's Peak

The 2003 Bishop's Peak Cabernet Sauvignon exhibits classic Cabernet aromas & flavors of cassis and currant with hints of anise & other fragrant spices.
The Cabernet Franc contributes hints of sweet cherry and olive.
This approachable Cabernet Sauvignon is perfect with the local signature dish, Santa Maria style BBQ: slow roasted top sirloin, charred on the outside & rare in the middle.

50 Recipes & glass of Wine

Peach & Arugula Salad

Ingredients

- 1 tablespoon balsamic vinegar
- 2 teaspoons fresh lemon juice
- 1/4 teaspoon salt (preferably sea salt)
- 3 tablespoons extra-virgin olive oil
- 4 firm-ripe peaches (11/2 lbs. total)
- 24 thin slices of pancetta (Italian un-smoked cured bacon; 11/4 lb.)
- 2 tablespoons olive oil
- 6 oz baby arugula (6 cups)
- 21/2 oz finely crumbled or puree ricotta
- Coarsely ground black pepper to taste

Chef Recommended Wine

Movia Ribolla Gialla

DIRECTIONS

Whisk together vinegar, lemon juice & salt; then add extra-virgin olive oil in a stream, whisking until emulsified.

Cut an X in bottom of each peach and immerse in boiling water 15 seconds; then transfer to a bowl of ice water.

Peel peaches and cut each into 6 wedges, then unroll pancetta slices and wrap one slice around each wedge, overlapping ends of pancetta . Heat remaining oil in 12" nonstick skillet over moderate heat until hot but not smoking; then cook peaches in 2 batches, turning occasionally with tongs, until pancetta is browned on all sides and cooked through, about 5 minutes per batch.

Transfer to a plate and keep warm, covered loosely with foil. Divide arugula and warm pancetta peaches among 8 salad plates. Drizzle with dressing and sprinkle with puree ricotta and pepper.
Serve immediately.

Question & Answer

What does "vintage" mean?

The vintage year on a wine label is the harvest year of the grapes from which the wine was made. The characteristics of a particular vintage year are determined by the weather conditions and resulting grape crop for that year. A California wine with a vintage date must be made from at least 95 percent of grapes harvested in the designated year.

Are there rules to knowing which vintages are better for which wine regions?

The characteristics of a particular vintage are determined by the quality of that year's grape crop. Improvements in wine making over the years have made vintage year less central to choosing a wine produced in most wine regions. Vintages are more important when collecting more expensive wines, especially those designed to be aged, and in growing regions where a less than satisfactory growing season is not compensated for using innovative wine making technology or practices. If you are interested in learning about specific vintages, reading wine publications and tasting wines from different vintages will help you determine a vintage's characteristics.

2003

Movia Ribolla Gialla

The Collio of Friuli becomes the Goriska hills across the border in Slovenia; Movia's vineyards straddle that border. Ales Kristancic farms his vines biodynamically. They may have managed the drought and heat of 2003 vintage more effectively than some of his neighbors' vines in Fruili. The wines produced from Ales Kristancic farms tastc fresh and succulent. It has lovely depth of citrusy fruit, with complexity from a slow native yeast fermentation & bright accents of chamomile, sorrel & thyme,

Penne with Roasted Butternut Squash & Mushrooms

Ingredients

- 2 cups butternut squash, peeled and cut into 1 inch cubes
- 2-3 tablespoons olive oil
- Salt
- 1 cup pancetta (1/4 inch dice)
- 1 cup onion, finely diced
- 2 tablespoons garlic, chopped
- 1 tablespoon crushed red pepper
- 2 cups mushrooms, sauté for 2 min
- 1/4 cup Italian parsley, chopped
- 1 pound penne
- Freshly grated Parmesan Cheese

Chef Recommended Wine

Valmar Cabernet Sauvignon

DIRECTIONS

Preheat oven to 350° F. Place the diced squash in a bowl, toss with 2 tbsp. of the olive oil & season with salt. Place the squash on a cookie sheet & roast for 20-25 minutes until the squash is tender and browned around the edges.

In a large sauté pan, heat the remaining olive oil & add the pancetta. Add the onion, garlic & sauté until golden brown, about 5-7 minutes. Add the crushed red pepper, mushrooms, & parsley. In a large pot, bring 2 gallons of water to a boil. Add the penne & salt & boil until the pasta is almost al dente. Drain the pasta, reserving 2 cups of the cooking liquid. Add the pasta & reserved cooking liquid to the sauté pan & sauté over high heat. Cook until the water half reduces & the pasta is al dente. Add the roasted squash & mushrooms, toss to heat the vegetables; taste for seasoning. Arrange pasta on platter & garnish with freshly grated Parmesan cheese.

Question & Answer

How about all of these rating systems, are some better than others?

The purpose of a wine rating is to quantify a wine's quality separate from those factors that influence price. Rating systems vary. Some rating systems are based on a 50 to 100-point scale, others on a 5-point scale, etc. Keep in mind when looking at ratings, that the evaluation of wine is subjective. Factors like bottle variability, tasting conditions, and the judges' likes and dislikes will influence a rating. You are the best judge of wine when it comes to what you enjoy drinking. Ratings can be used as a helpful guideline for choosing a wine once you are familiar with the rater's preferred style (if an individual) or
the preferred style of those judges whose opinions contribute to a rating.

Where does cork come from?

Corks are produced from the bark of a tree grown in the western Mediterranean. It is unique in that it can be peeled from the tree without hurting the tree.

2000

Valmar Cabernet Sauvignon

It is common to find mixtures of grapes in red and white wines, such as Cabernet-Merlot or Chenin-Colombard.
The purpose of these mixtures is to combine and balance the flavors and aromas of different varieties into a must.

50 Recipes & glass of Wine

Pork Chops with Mustard Cream Sauce

Ingredients

- 2 lbs. Pork chops
- Fresh sage leaves
- 1 bottle white wine
- 4 sprigs rosemary
- 4 Tbsp. Extra Virgin olive oil
- 1 cup mustard
- 1 cup milk
- Salt & pepper

DIRECTIONS

Place the pork chop meat into a bowl, cover with wine and marinate for 2 days in a cool place. Remove the pork from the marinade, dry it and let it brown on all sides in a casserole with the butter. Remove pork from casserole and set aside in a warm place.

In a frying pan add a cup of mustard, and a cup of milk. Add salt & pepper, sage leaves & rosemary and let it cook slowly until it is reduced as a sauce. Remove from heat and strain. Place the pork chop on a plate and cover with the reduced sauce.

Serve with mashed potatoes or couscous.

Chef Recommended Wine

Notarpanaro
Salento Rosso
Taurino

Question & Answer

Why is cork used to stop wine bottles?

Cork is used to stop wine bottles because its structure renders it light, elastic, and impermeable to most liquids and gases. Corks are produced using the bark of cork trees grown in the western Mediterranean.

What is a kosher wine?

A wine is kosher if it is made using strict rabbinical production techniques. A kosher wine cannot include any chemical additives, gelatin, lactose, glycerin, corn products or non-wine yeasts. In addition, Sabbath-observing Jews must conduct the entire wine making process under rabbinical supervision. Kosher wines are produced by wineries all over the world.

What is a dessert wine?

A dessert wine is usually a sweet wine drunk at or for dessert. Due to its sweetness it is drunk in smaller quantities than table wine. In the U.S., the classification of dessert wine is that of wines which are fortified (the addition of brandy or other spirits to raise the level of alcohol in the wine) whether they are sweet or dry.

1999

Notarpanaro
Salento Rosso
Taurino

It is deep red, very full bodied, strong and intense. There is an unmistakable hint of port in the taste and nose. It's definitely worth a try.

Spaghetti Primavera

Ingredients

- 1/2 stick of butter
- 1 medium onion, minced
- 1 clove garlic, minced
- 1 lb thin asparagus
- 1/2 lb. sliced mushrooms (cut in 1/4 slices)
- 6 oz. broccoli (small florets)
- 1 medium red pepper
- 1 large carrot, thin slices
- 1 cup green peas
- 2 tbsp. chopped basil
- Salt & pepper
- 1 cup grated Romano cheese
- 1 lb. Spaghetti, cooked & drained

DIRECTIONS

Vegetables may be prepared in advance and refrigerated. Heat wok or deep skillet over medium heat. Add butter, onion, garlic & sauté until onions are softened, for 2 minutes. Mix in asparagus, mushrooms, red pepper, broccoli, & carrots; stir-fry for 2 minutes.

Increase heat to high. Season to taste with salt & pepper. Add pasta, toss with vegetables, and add cheese.

Garnish plate with fresh parsley.

It is best to let pasta primavera sit in pot for about 30 minutes. Serve.

Chef Recommended Wine

Tobin James "Made in the Shade" Merlot

Question & Answer

Why are some wines white, some red, and some pink?
White wines are generally made with grapes with yellow or green skins. White wines can also be made from black-skinned grapes if the juice is separated from the grape skins early enough-i.e., before fermentation. Red wines get their color from being fermented in contact with the skins of dark grapes. Rosé gets its pink color by either a short contact time with the skins of dark-colored grapes before fermentation or by mixing finished red wine with finished white

What are sulfites and should I be worried about them?
Sulfite is a term used to describe sulfur dioxide and other sulfur derivatives. Sulfites are found in all wines, as they are a natural product of fermentation. Sulfur dioxide is used in wine making to prevent oxidation, kill bacteria and wild yeasts, and encourage quick and clean fermentation. The U.S. government requires wine labels to include "Contains Sulfites" to alert those who may be allergic to sulfites. Approximately 1% of the population is allergic to sulfites.

2004

Tobin James "Made in the Shade" Merlot

This Merlot from the Paso Robles area of California, has all the qualities that made Merlot famous; delicious blackberry jam and plum flavors with a luscious mouth like a soft velvety texture. Uncomplicated and so easy to drink, "Made in the shade" Merlot is one of Tobin James most popular and hard to find wines.

Cheese Ravioli with Green Peas

Ingredients

- 2 lbs. Fresh cheese ravioli
- 1 tablespoon olive oil
- 1 lb. Roma tomatoes, peeled, seeded & chopped
- 1 cup green peas
- 1 tablespoon fresh parsley
- 1 tablespoon fresh basil
- 1/4 cup chopped green onions
- 3 cloves garlic, crushed
- 1/2 teaspoon salt
- 1/2 teaspoon freshly ground pepper
- 2 Tbsp. Grated Parmesan cheese

Chef Recommended Wine

Vernaccia di San Gimignano Terre di Tufi

DIRECTIONS

Cook ravioli according to package directions. While pasta is cooking, prepare the sauce. In a large nonstick skillet, heat 1 Tbsp. oil over a medium-high flame. Add tomatoes, green peas, parsley, garlic, and salt & pepper. Cook 2 to 3 minutes, stirring occasionally until vegetables are warmed through. Remove from heat. Drain pasta well. Transfer to a large bowl, and toss with 1 teaspoon oil. Add half of the sauce to the ravioli; toss gently, but thoroughly to mix. Transfer the ravioli to a large serving platter.

Pour remaining sauce over ravioli.

Garnish with Parmesan cheese.

Question & Answer

Is wine fattening?

The calories in a 4-ounce glass of wine ranges from about 80 to 100 calories. Lighter wines tend to have fewer calories than heavier wines. Some wines are higher in carbohydrates than others due to their residual sugars. For example, a dry Sauvignon Blanc may have 2 grams of carbohydrate where as a very sweet dessert wine could have up to 12 grams. Wine is fat free and contains no cholesterol.

Why do some wines give you a headache?

Histamines, found in the skins of grapes, seem to give some people headaches if they are sensitive to histamines. Red wine will affect a histamine sensitive wine drinker more than white wine because red wine has spent more time in contact with grape skins.

I've heard that drinking wine, especially red wine, is good for me. Is this true?

There has been more and more consensus in the last few years within the scientific community and governmental and public health circles that moderate wine consumption is in fact associated with a number of positive health outcomes.

2003

Vernaccia di San Gimignano Terre di Tufi

Vernaccia is one of Italy's oldest grapes. This version from a 235 acre vineyard near Tuscany's famed "city of towers" is not aromatically intense but it does offer nice melon and floral tones. Tart and flinty in the mouth.

50 Recipes & glass of Recipes &

Risotto with Mushrooms

Ingredients

- 3 Tbsp. finely chopped onions
- 3 Tbsp. olive oil
- 1 Tbsp. Chopped parsley
- 1 Tbsp. Chopped celery
- 1 clove garlic, peeled
- Salt & pepper
- 10 ozs. Fresh mushrooms, sliced thin
- 1 cup milk
- 1-1/2 cups Italian Arborio rice
- 4 Tbsp. Cream
- 5 cups hot meat broth
- 1 Tbsp. Butter
- 1 cup freshly grated Parmigiano-Reggiano

DIRECTIONS

In a casserole over medium-high heat, sauté the onion and the garlic in the oil. Add the parsley, celery, salt & pepper. Discard the garlic when it becomes colored a pale brown.

After about 5 minutes, add the mushrooms, and cook over low heat.

Stir frequently and add the milk to keep the mushrooms tender, and then add the rice and cream.

Cook the rice by adding the hot meat broth, a ladleful at a time, putting in a fresh ladleful as the broth evaporates, while stirring continuously.
When the rice is cooked, after about 25 minutes, add the butter and Parmigiano Reggiano and serve immediately.

Chef Recommended Wine

Nu Har D'avola
Cabernet Sauvignon

Question & Answer

How is wine made?

The following is a synopsis of the basic steps taken to make wine: Grapes are crushed to release the sugar in their juice. The juice naturally ferments when yeast comes in contact with the sugar in the grape juice. The result is alcohol and carbon dioxide. Red wine is made with dark-skinned grapes and fermented with the grape skins. White wines are made with white grapes, or if made with some dark-skinned grapes the grape skins are removed prior to fermentation. Rosé wines have contact with the skins of dark-skinned grapes just long enough to impart a pink color. The fermented wine is then separated from the grape solids and transferred into a vat or casks where it is clarified, stabilized, and may be taken though optional processes. Finally, the wine is bottled.

What is malolactic fermentation?

A natural process during which beneficial bacteria convert the malic (very tart) acid in a wine to lactic (softer tasting) acid. Malolactic fermentation can take place on its own or be prompted by the winemaker.

Is European wine better than wine made here in the U.S.? Although wines from different regions will vary in style, quality wines are produced all over the world. Each wine region may produce many types of wine, but most likely specialize and excel in a few due to weather and growing conditions.

2004

Nu Har D'avola Cabernet Sauvignon

The 2003 Nuhar is a ripe, open textured wine with early appeal. Though young, it is already drinking beautifully, and provides an ideal accompaniment to hearty meals such as pastas and roasts.

50 Recipes & a glass of Wine

Roast Beef Loin

Ingredients

- 1 (2-3lb.) Boneless beef loin fat trimmed
- 2 cloves of garlic
- 2 teaspoons fresh thyme
- 2 teaspoons fresh sage
- 4 teaspoons olive oil
- 4 teaspoons salt
- 1 tsp. black peppercorns

DIRECTIONS

Drop garlic into processor; blend until finely chopped. Add sage, thyme, oil, black pepper, peppercorn and salt; process until paste forms.
Pat meat dry with paper towels. Rub meat all over with herb paste. Cover; chill at least 3 hours. Preheat oven to 450°F.

Place meat, side up, on rack in roasting pan. Roast meat 15 minutes. Reduce oven temperature to 350°F. Roast meat until thermometer inserted into thickest part of meat registers 130°F for medium-rare, about 35 minutes (or 140°F for medium, about 40 minutes).

Remove from oven; let meat stand for 20 minutes.

Cut crosswise into 1/3 inch thick slices.

Arrange slices on platter.

Chef Recommended Wine

Bruno Rocca
Rabaya

2001

*Bruno Rocca
Rabaya*

This is always one of the best from Barbaresco, and deservedly. Aromas of very ripe raspberries & blackberries with a hint of cedar. Full-bodied, with silky tannins & a long, long finish. This is refined and structured.

Rosemary Grilled Chicken

Ingredients

- 1 whole chicken
- 1 orange
- 1/3 cup white wine vinegar
- 1/4 cup Extra Virgin Olive Oil
- 1 tablespoon fresh rosemary, chopped
- 1/4 teaspoon black pepper

DIRECTIONS

With kitchen scissors or chef''s knife, cut along each side of chicken''s backbone; remove backbone and trim visible fat.

Tuck wing tips behind back; flatten to 1 layer. Place in shallow casserole.

Grate orange rind and squeeze out juice; mix with vinegar, oil, rosemary & pepper.

Pour over chicken; cover and marinate in refrigerator, turning often, for at least 4 hours or up to 24 hours.

Reserving marinade, place chicken, skin side down, on greased grill over medium low indirect heat. Add soaked wood chips. Cover and cook for 1 hour, turning and basting with marinade halfway through.

Transfer to direct heat; cook for 10 minutes per side or until meat thermometer inserted in thigh registers 185 • F. Remove to platter and tent with foil; let stand for 10 minutes before cutting into quarters.

Chef Recommended Wine

Chionetti Dolcetto di Dogliani Briccollero

Glossary of Wine Terms

Acidity: A naturally occurring component of every wine; the level of perceived sharpness; a key element to a wine's longevity; a leading determinant of balance.

Alcohol: The end product of fermentation; technically ethyl alcohol resulting from the interaction of natural grape sugars and yeast; generally above 12.5% in dry table wines.

Alsace: A highly regarded wine region in eastern France renowned for dry and sweet wines made from Riesling, Gewürztraminer, Pinot Blanc, Pinot Gris and others.

Amarone: A succulent higher-alcohol red wine hailing from the Veneto region in northern Italy; made primarily from Corvina grapes dried on racks before pressing.

AOC: Appellation d'Origine Contrôlée, a French term for a denominated, governed wine region such as Margaux or Nuits-St.-Georges.

Aroma: A scent that's a component of the bouquet or nose; i.e. cherry is an aromatic component of a fruity bouquet.

AVA: American Viticultural Area; a denominated American wine region approved by the Bureau of Alcohol, Tobacco and Firearms.

Bacchus: The Roman god of wine, known as Dionysus in ancient Greece; a hybrid white grape from Germany.

2004

Chionetti Dolcetto di Dogliani Briccollero

Very distinctive, with ripe berry, wet earth and a hint of sous-bois. Medium-bodied, with a fresh palate and intense finish. Loads of character here.

Salmon with Gorgonzola Cheese

Ingredients

- 4 salmon fillets
- 4 large cablage leaves
- 5 oz. Gorgonzola cheese
- Fresh thyme
- Sage
- Chervil
- Salt & pepper

DIRECTIONS

Salt & pepper the salmon fillets; wrap them in the cabbage leaves and steam them.
Remove from the steamer and place them on a baking dish. Mince the fresh herbs and sprinkle over each piece of salmon.
Add Gorgonzola cheese. Bake the salmon in oven at 350° for 10 minutes or until the Gorgonzola has melted.

Chef Recommended Wine

Santa Margherita
Pinot Grigio

Glossary of Wine Terms

Balance: The level of harmony between acidity, tannins, fruit, oak, and other elements in a wine; a perceived quality that is more individual than scientific.

Barrel Fermented: A process by which wine (usually white) is fermented in oak barrels rather than in stainless steel tanks; a richer, creamier, oakier style of wine.

Barrique: French for "barrel", generally a barrel of 225 liters.

Beaujolais: A juicy, flavorful red wine made from Gamay grapes grown in the region of the same name.

Beaujolais Nouveau: The first Beaujolais wine of the harvest; its annual release date is the third Thursday in November.

Blanc de Blancs: The name for Champagne made entirely from Chardonnay grapes.

Blanc de Noirs: The name for Champagne made entirely from red grapes, either Pinot Noir or Pinot Meunier, or both.

Blend: The process whereby two or more grape varieties are combined after separate fermentation; common blends include Côtes de Rhône and red and white Bordeaux.

Blush: A wine made from red grapes but which appears pink or salmon in color because the grape skins were removed from the fermenting juice before more color could be imparted; more commonly referred to as rosé.

2005

Santa Margherita Pinot Grigio

This dry white wine is pale straw-yellow in color. The clean, intense aroma and dry flavor with pleasant golden apple aftertaste make Santa Margherita Pinot Grigio a wine of great character and versatility.

50 Recipes & glass of Wine

Salmon Puttenesca

Ingredients

- 6 tablespoons olive oil

- 2 cloves of garlic, peeled & minced

- 2 ounces or more of black kalamata olives, pitted & chopped

- 1 teaspoon coarsely chopped capers

- 1 large fresh tomato, peeled & coarsely chopped

- 4 or 5 anchovy fillets, chopped

- 4 6-ounce salmon fillets

- Freshly ground pepper to taste

- 1 cup all-purpose flour for dredging Garnishes

- Salt & freshly ground pepper

- Chopped parsley

- 1 teaspoon red pepper flakes

DIRECTIONS

Heat a large frying pan and add 3 tablespoons of the oil and the garlic. Sauté the garlic until golden brown.
Add the olives, capers, tomato, and anchovy fillets.
Stir well and heat through for about 6 minutes.

Season the salmon with black pepper. Roll each fillet in flour and pat off the excess flour. Heat another large frying pan and add remaining 3 tablespoons of oil.

Sauté the fish over medium heat about 2 minutes on each side. The fish should be lightly browned but not overcooked!

Top the fish with the sauce, season to taste, and garnish with chopped parsley and optional red pepper flakes.
Serves 4

Chef Recommended Wine

Von Buhl Armand
Kabinett Riesling

Glossary of Wine Terms

Bodega: Spanish for winery; literally the "room where barrels are stored."

Body: The impression of weight on one's palate; light, medium and full are common body qualifiers.

Bordeaux: A city on the Garonne River in southwest France; a large wine-producing region with more than a dozen subregions; a red wine made mostly from Cabernet Sauvignon, Merlot and Cabernet Franc; a white wine made from Sauvignon Blanc and Sémillon.

Botrytis Cinerea: A beneficial mold that causes grapes to shrivel and sugars to concentrate, resulting in sweet, unctuous wines; common botrytis wines include Sauternes, Tokay and German beerenauslese.

Bouquet: The sum of a wine's aromas; how a wine smells as a whole; a key determinant of quality.

Breathe: The process of letting a wine open up via the introduction of air.

Brix: A scale used to measure the level of sugar in unfermented grapes. Multiplying brix by .55 will yield a wine's future alcohol level.

Brut: A French term used to describe the driest Champagnes.

2004

Von Buhl Armand Kabinett Riesling

Plenty of citrus notes here ~ lime & grapefruit ~ and snappy acidity tp support them, and a second wave of intensity that persists through the finish.

Sausages @ Broccoletti

Ingredients

- 2 lbs. fresh sweet pork sausages
- 1 small red chile pepper
- 6 lbs. Broccoletti (rabe)
- 6 Tbsp. olive oil
- 4 cloves garlic

DIRECTIONS

Prick the sausages with a fork so they don't burst while cooking. Heat 1 Tbsp. olive oil and sauté the sausages over a medium flame. When they get a color, add 1/2 cup of water and continue to cook for 12 minutes. Remove from heat and set aside. Clean the broccoli discarding the hard stems.

Heat the remainder of the oil in a large casserole. Add the garlic and 1 chile pepper. Remove the garlic when brown and add broccoletti.

Sauté over medium heat, for 20 minutes with the casserole covered, stirring occasionally. Add the sausages and cook for another 5 minutes with the pot uncovered. Remove from heat and serve.

Chef Recommended Wine

Dolcetto d'Alba
Vignalunga

Glossary of Wine Terms

Burgundy: A prominent French wine region stretching from Chablis in the north to Lyons in the south; Pinot Noir is the grape for red Burgundy, Chardonnay for white.

Cabernet Franc: A red grape common to Bordeaux; characteristics include an herbal, leafy flavor and a soft, fleshy texture.

Cabernet Sauvignon: A powerful, tannic red grape of noble heritage; the base grape for many red Bordeaux and most of the best red wines from California, Washington, Chile and South Africa; capable of aging for decades.

Cap: Grape solids like pits, skins and stems that rise to the top of a tank during fermentation; what gives red wines color, tannins and weight.

Cava: Spanish for "cellar", but also a Spanish sparkling wine made in the traditional Champagne style from Xarello, Macabeo and Parellada grapes.

Chablis: A town and wine region east of Paris known for steely, minerally Chardonnay.

Champagne: A denominated region northeast of Paris in which Chardonnay, Pinot Noir and Pinot Meunier grapes are made into sparkling wine.

Chaptalization: The process of adding sugar to fermenting grapes in order to increase alcohol.

2004

Dolcetto d'Alba Vignalunga

This wine has a deep, ruby red hue with purple reflections and an intense nose to match, filled with delicate aromas of ripe red fruits and violets. Dry and full-bodied on the palate, it feels soft in the mouth, with harmonious and intense flavors.
The finish is long and strong, with a pleasantly bitter note on the aftertaste.

50 Recipes & glass of Wine

Seafood Chowder

Ingredients

- 2 Tbsp. bacon drippings
- 2 tablespoons butter
- 4 white onions
- 2 celery ribs diced
- 2 lbs. mixed seafood
- 1 lb. Crab meat
- 2 cups potatoes
- 2 tomatoes, diced
- 1 small yellow zucchini, diced
- 1 small green zucchini, diced
- 2 cups green peas
- 1 cup sweet peppers, all colors
- 4 Tbsp. Flour
- 6 cups milk
- Milk to thin
- Salt & pepper to taste
- Tomato sauce/soup to taste

DIRECTIONS

Melt bacon fat and butter in heavy saucepan over medium-low heat. Add onions and sauté until clear.

Add celery and cook gently for about 5 minutes.

Add seafood products and sauté in saucepan at medium high heat to coat, flavor and brown slightly.

Add flour and milk, stirring well to avoid lumps.

Add remaining ingredients, except peas, in order of required cooking time (potatoes, zucchini, tomatoes, peppers, etc.).

Add wine and season to taste. Heat until heated through, but do not boil.

Add peas about 20 minutes before serving.

Use milk to thin as necessary.

Chef Recommended Wine

Kali Hart
Chardonnay

Glossary of Wine Terms

Chardonnay: Arguably the best and most widely planted white wine grape in the world.

Château: French for "castle", an estate with its own vineyards.

Chenin Blanc: A white grape common in the Loire Valley of France.

Chianti: A scenic, hilly section of Tuscany known for fruity red wines made mostly from Sangiovese grapes.

Claret: An English name for red Bordeaux.

Clos: Pronounced "Cloh", this French word once applied only to vineyards surrounded by walls.

Color: A key determinant of a wine's age and quality; white wines grow darker in color as they age while red wines turn brownish orange.

Cooperative: A winery owned jointly by multiple grape growers.

Corked: A wine with musty, mushroomy aromas and flavors resulting from a cork tainted by TCA (trichloroanisol).

Crianza: A Spanish term for a red wine that has been aged in oak barrels for at least one year.

2005

Kali Hart
Chardonnay

The 2005 Kali Hart Chardonnay is medium straw in appearance with great clarity and brillance. The nose displays intense tropical fruit of papaya, melon & nectarine. In the mouth this wine is concentrated & intense with explosive pineapple, white peach & Pippin apple flavors framed by vibrant acidity.

Shrimp Fettuccine

Ingredients

- 1/2 stick of butter
- 1/2 medium bell pepper
- 1 medium onion
- 1 stick of celery
- 2 cloves of garlic
- 1/4 cup of parsley
- 2 lbs. Shrimp (peeled & cleaned)
- 1 teaspoon of chile pepper
- 1 cup tomato sauce
- 12 oz. fettuccine

DIRECTIONS

Boil fettuccine. Cut up onion, bell pepper & celery. Put butter in pan and sauté bell pepper, onion, celery, & garlic.

Add shrimp and cook until shrimp are pink. Add tomato sauce.

Pour shrimp sauce over fettuccine and sauté.

Sprinkle parsley.

Chef Recommended Wine

Rumball
Sparkling Shiraz

Glossary of Wine Terms

Cru: A French term for ranking a wine's inherent quality, i.e. cru bourgeois, cru classé, premier cru and grand cru.

Decant: The process of transferring wine from a bottle to another holding vessel. The purpose is generally to aerate a young wine or to separate an older wine from any sediment.

Denominación de Origen: Spanish for "appellation of origin"; like the French AOC or Italian DOC.

Denominazione di Origine Controllata: Italian for a controlled wine region; similar to the French AOC or Spanish DO.

Disgorge: The process by which final sediments are removed from traditionally made sparkling wines prior to the adding of the dosage.

Dosage: A sweetened spirit added at the very end to Champagne and other traditionally made sparkling wines. It determines whether a wine is brut, extra dry, dry or semisweet.

Douro: A river in Portugal as well as the wine region famous for producing Port wines.

Dry: A wine containing no more than 0.2 percent unfermented sugar.

Earthy: A term used to describe aromas and flavors that have a certain soil-like quality.

Rumball
Sparkling Shiraz

The Sparkling Shiraz is elegant with full fruit & strong Shiraz varietal character. It has a soft, smooth palate & is a great wine to complement fully flavored foods.

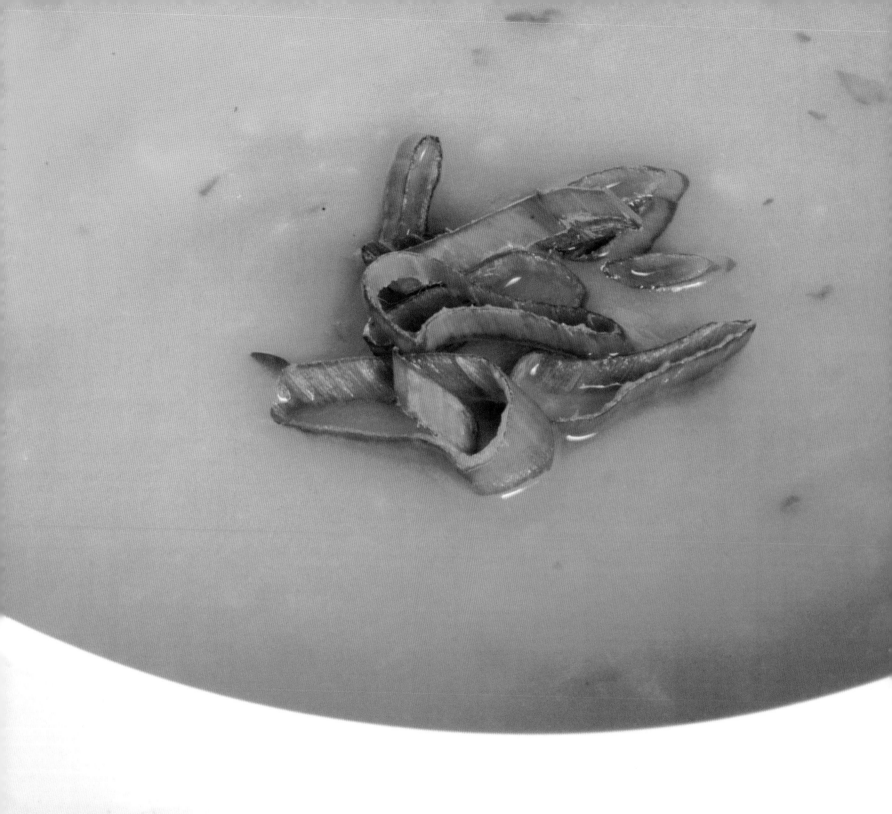

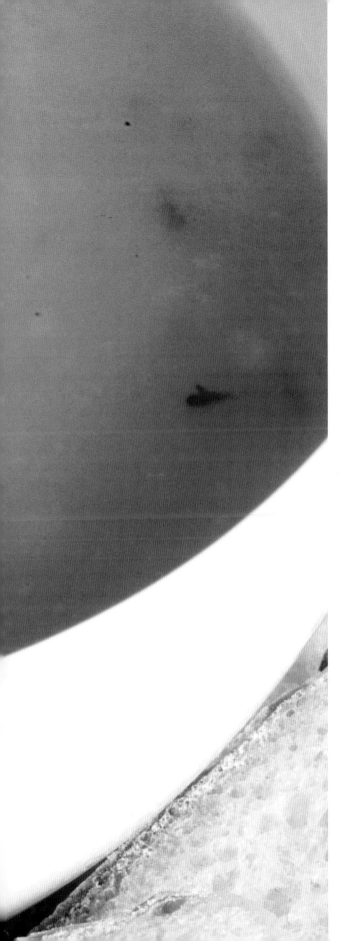

Squash Soup

Ingredients

- 3 acorn squash, halved lengthwise & seeded
- 1 onion, chopped
- 3 cups vegetable broth
- 1-1/2 cups heavy whipping cream
- 2 tablespoons butter
- Salt & black pepper to taste

DIRECTIONS

Preheat oven to 325ºF. Place the squash, cut sides down, in a baking dish. Add 1/4 inch water in baking dish, cover with foil and bake 35-40 minutes or until tender. Cool.

In a large saucepan, melt butter.

Add onion and cook over low heat, stirring occasionally until the onion is softened but not brown.

Scrape the squash out of the flesh and add to onions. Add the stock and heavy cream. Cook over moderate heat, stirring occasionally, about 25 minutes.

Puree the soup in a blender or food processor.

Season with salt and pepper to taste and serve.

Chef Recommended Wine

Chateau de Pampelonne

50 Recipes & glass of Wine   173

Glossary of Wine Terms

Enology: The science of wine production; an enologist is a professional winemaker; an enophile is someone who enjoys wine.

Fermentation: The process by which sugar is transformed into alcohol; how grape juice interacts with yeast to become wine.

Filtration: The process by which wine is clarified before bottling.

Fining: Part of the clarification process whereby elements are added to the wine, i.e. egg whites, in order to capture solids prior to filtration.

Fortified Wine: A wine in which brandy is introduced during fermentation; sugars and sweetness are high due to the suspended fermentation.

Fumé Blanc: A name created by Robert Mondavi to describe dry Sauvignon Blanc.

Gamay: A red grape exceedingly popular in the Beaujolais region of France.

Gewürztraminer: A sweet and spicy white grape popular in eastern France, Germany, Austria, northern Italy and California.

Graft: A vineyard technique in which the bud-producing part of a grapevine is attached to an existing root.

Gran Reserva: A Spanish term used for wines that are aged in wood and bottles for at least five years prior to release.

2003

Chateau de Pampelonne

The bright, crisp mouth is elegant with full fruit and strong Shiraz varietal cgaracter. It has a soft, smooth palate and is a great wine to complement fully flavored foods.

Sirloin Steak

Ingredients

- 1 boneless Sirloin Steak
- Salt & pepper to taste
- 1 Tbsp. Olive oil
- 1 clove garlic, minced or crushed
- 1/4 teaspoon black pepper
- 3 tablespoons red wine
- 1 tablespoon butter

DIRECTIONS

Once the steak has cooked, you need to work fast to finish this dish! For best results, assemble & measure out all the ingredients before cooking the steak!

Pat steak dry. In large skillet, heat oil over medium-high heat and cook steak for about 4 minutes on each side to achieve a doneness of medium. Once cooked to desired doneness, lightly season with salt and ground pepper, then transfer steak to platter and keep warm. Add garlic, pepper; sauté for 10 seconds. Add wine & boil until almost all liquid is evaporated. Bring to a simmer, stirring. Add butter and stir over low heat until melted. Spoon sauce over steak and serve with sliced baked potato & broccoli. Garnish with red & yellow Julienne cut bell pepper.

Chef Recommended Wine

Massolino
Barolo

Glossary of Wine Terms

Grand Cru: French for "great growth"; the very best vineyards.

Green: A term used to describe underripe, vegetal flavors in a wine.

Grenache: A hearty, productive red grape popular in southern France as well as in Spain, where it is called Garnacha.

Grüner Veltliner: A white grape popular in Austria that makes lean, fruity, racy wines.

Haut: A French word meaning "high." It applies to quality as well as altitude.

Hectare: A metric measure equal to 10,000 square meters or 2.47 acres.

Hectoliter: A metric measure equal to 100 liters or 26.4 gallons.

Herbaceous: An aroma or flavor similar to green; often an indication of underripe grapes or fruit grown in a cool climate.

Hollow: A term used to describe a wine that doesn't have depth or body.

Hybrid: The genetic crossing of two or more grape types; common hybrids include Müller-Thurgau and Bacchus.

2001

Massolino
Barolo

Aromas of plums & hints of meat with berries.
Full-bodied, with soft, round tannins & a long, long finish. Slightly one dimensional, but clearly outstanding. Always a great value. Well made.

50 Recipes & glass of Wine

Grilled Swordfish in a Lemon & Tarragon Sauce

Ingredients

- 1/2 cup Italian salad dressing
- 1/4 cup lemon juice
- 1 tablespoon Dijon mustard
- 2 tsp. dried tarragon leaves, crushed
- 1 tsp. freeze dried chives, chopped
- 1 teaspoon lemon peel, grated
- 1/8 teaspoon white pepper
- 1 to 1 1/2 lbs. Swordfish fillets, 1" thick

DIRECTIONS

Mix all ingredients except fish. Pour over fish.

Marinate in refrigerator 2 hours.

Drain, reserving marinade.

Place fish on greased rack of broiler pan or grill. Broil or grill over low coals, uncovered, brushing frequently on both sides with reserved marinade.

Cooking time: 15 minutes.

Chef Recommended Wine

Lugana di Frati

Glossary of Wine Terms

Ice Wine: From the German eiswein, this is a wine made from frozen grapes; Germany, Austria and Canada are leading ice wine producers.

Jeroboam: An oversized bottle equal to six regular 750ml bottles.

Kabinett: A German term for a wine of quality; usually the driest of Germany's best Rieslings.

Kosher: A wine made according to strict Jewish rules under rabbinical supervision.

Labrusca: Grape types native to North America such as Concord and Catawba.

Late Harvest: A term used to describe dessert wines made from grapes left on the vines for an extra long period, often until botrytis has set in.

Lees: Heavy sediment left in the barrel by fermenting wines; a combination of spent yeast cells and grape solids.

Legs: A term used to describe how wine sticks to the inside of a wineglass after drinking or swirling.

Loire: A river in central France as well as a wine region famous for Chenin Blanc, Sauvignon Blanc and Cabernet Franc.

2004

Lugana di Frati

The nose is clean, delicate and fragrant, with perfumes of fresh white flowers and nettles, apricots and almonds.
An attractive acidity gives it an elegant finish and makes it particularly easy to drink.
It is a perfect match for cold starters, vegetable soups and steamed or grilled fish.

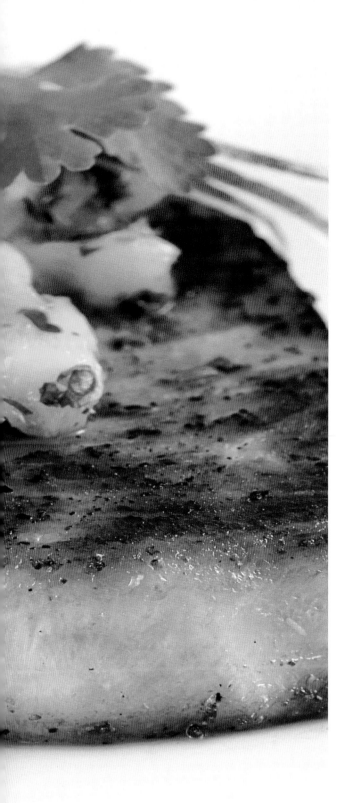

Grilled Swordfish with Mango Sauce

Ingredients

- 1/2 cup Extra Virgin Olive Oil
- 1 teaspoon black pepper
- 4 cloves garlic, minced
- 1 shallot, chopped fine
- 3 tablespoons cilantro, chopped
- 4 5 ounce swordfish steaks

DIRECTIONS

Mix all ingredients and marinate fish for 1 hour.
Pan-fried over medium heat for 3 minutes on each side, or until done.

Mango Sauce
Peel and seed fresh mangoes, approximately 2 pounds cut into small cubes in a bowl.

Mix extra virgin olive oil, black pepper, salt & cilantro.
Mix and pour over fish.

Serves 4

Chef Recommended Wine

Jermann
Vintage Tunina

Glossary of Wine Terms

Maceration: The process of allowing grape juice and skins to ferment together, thereby imparting color, tannins and aromas.

Madeira: A fortified wine that has been made on a Portuguese island off the coast of Morocco since the 15th century.

Maderized: Stemming from the word Madeira, this term means oxidization in a hot environment.

Magnum: A bottle equal to two regular 750ml bottles. Malbec: A hearty red grape of French origin now exceedingly popular in Argentina.

Malolactic Fermentation: A secondary fermentation, often occurring in barrels, whereby harsher malic acid is converted into creamier lactic acid.

Médoc: A section of Bordeaux on the west bank of the Gironde Estuary known for great red wines; Margaux, St.-Estèphe and Pauillac are three leading AOCs in the Médoc.

Merlot: A lauded red grape popular in Bordeaux and throughout the world; large amounts of Merlot exist in Italy, the United States, South America and elsewhere.

Must: Crushed grapes about to go or going through fermentation.

Nebbiolo: A red grape popular in the Piedmont region of northwest Italy; the grape that yields both Barolo and Barbaresco.

2003

Jermann
Vintage Tunina

Chardonnay, Saufignon, Ribolla, Malvasia & the rare Picolit grapes in this wine; from late-harvested fruit.

Tuna Macaroni Bean Potato Salad

Ingredients

- 1 cup uncooked elbow macaroni
- 3 cups string beans
- 1 cup boiled potatoes
- 1 can (6.5 oz.) Tuna, drained & flaked
- 1/2 cup chopped celery
- 1/2 cup chopped onion
- 1/2 cup mayonnaise
- 1 Tbsp. Honey mustard
- 2 Tbsp. extra virgin olive oil

DIRECTIONS

Cook macaroni according to package directions, drain; rinse under cold water and drain.

Combine macaroni with next five ingredients.

Combine mayonnaise, mustard, salt, black pepper and mix well.

Pour over macaroni mixture and toss gently.

Cover; chill at least one hour.

Serve salad on lettuce and garnish with tomato wedges and parsley.

Chef Recommended Wine

Riesling
Loosen Bros

Glossary of Wine Terms

Négociant: A French term for a person or company that buys wines from others and then labels it under his or her own name; stems from the French word for "shipper".

Nose: Synonymous with bouquet; the sum of a wine's aromas.
Oaky: A term used to describe woody aromas and flavors; butter, popcorn and toast notes are found in "oaky" wines.

Organic: Grapes grown without the aid of chemical-based fertilizers, pesticides or herbicides.

Oxidized: A wine that is no longer fresh because it was exposed to too much air.

PH: An indication of a wine's acidity expressed by how much hydrogen is in it.

Phylloxera: A voracious vine louse that over time has destroyed vineyards in Europe and California.

Piedmont: An area in northwest Italy known for Barolo, Barbaresco, Barbera, Dolcetto and Moscato.

Pinot Blanc: A white grape popular in Alsace, Germany and elsewhere.

Pinot Gris: Also called Pinot Grigio, this is a grayish-purple grape that yields a white wine with a refreshing character.

2005

Riesling Loosen Bros

This clear, light straw-color wine offers a fresh, clean scent of ripe pears.It's fruity pear juice on the palate too, juicy and fresh, with just a touch of sweetnees well balanced by zippy acidity; there's a prickly hint of barely perceptible carbonation on the tongue.

50 Recipes & glass of Wine

Veal Saltimbocca

Ingredients

- 1 lb. top round veal
- 1/4 lb. sliced prosciutto
- Fresh sage leaves
- 1 cup flour
- 1/2 cup beef broth (optional)
- 2 tablespoons olive oil
- 4 tablespoons butter
- 1 glass white wine
- Salt & pepper

DIRECTIONS

Cut the veal into thin slices and flatten with a wooden mallet. Place a slice of ham over each slice of meat with a sage leaf in the center.

Put the oil & butter in a saucepan.

Lightly dust the veal with flour & sauté over medium flame for 3 minutes. Add wine and simmer for another 2 minutes. Add salt & pepper to taste.

Arrange the veal on a serving platter. In the skillet used to cook the veal, let the cooking juices reduce for a minute, then pour over the veal saltimbocca. Serve immediately.

Garnish with parsley over a bed of mashed potatoes.

Chef Recommended Wine

Campofiorin
Rosso del
Veronese Ripasso

Glossary of Wine Terms

Pinot Noir: The prime red grape of Burgundy, Champagne and Oregon.

Pinotage: A hybrid between Pinot Noir and Cinsault that's grown almost exclusively in South Africa.

Plonk: A derogatory name for cheap, poor-tasting wine.

Pomace: The mass of skins, pits, and stems left over after fermentation; used to make grappa in Italy and marc in France.

Port: A sweet, fortified wine made in the Douro Valley of Portugal and aged in the coastal town of Vila Nova de Gaia; variations include Vintage, Tawny, Late Bottled Vintage, Ruby, White and others.

Premier Cru: French for "first growth"; a high-quality vineyard but one not as good as grand cru.

Press: The process by which grape juice is extracted prior to fermentation; a machine that extracts juice from grapes.

Primeur (en): A French term for wine sold while it is sill in the barrels; known as "futures" in English-speaking countries.

Pruning: The annual vineyard chore of trimming back plants from the previous harvest.

Racking: The process of moving wine from barrel to barrel, while leaving sediment behind.

2003

Campofiorin Rosso del Veronese Ripasso

It is a classic "supervenetian red". It demonstrates the outstanding character of local grapes, & uniqueness of its production method. Campofiorin is deliberately made to be a wine with good drinkability & to combine both power & structure at the same time.

Veal Tenderloin with Peppercorn Sauce

Ingredients

- 2 lb. Veal Tenderloin
- 1 teaspoon, Fresh Rosemary, chopped
- 1 teaspoon, Fresh Thyme, chopped
- 1 teaspoon, Fresh Basil, chopped
- 1 teaspoon, Fresh Shallots, chopped
- 1 teaspoon, Fresh Clove of Garlic, crushed
- 1 lb. of butter
- Pinch of Kosher Salt
- 2 teaspoons, 5 peppercorns, roughly cracked
- 2 oz Apple Brandy

DIRECTIONS

Rub veal with thyme, rosemary, basil, salt & 5 peppercorns. Pan-sear the veal ~ keeping the temperature high, the veal will sear golden brown and eventually release itself from sticking to the pan.

Brown all sides ~ leaving the center pink/rare. Place in oven at 360° F for 10 minutes. Remove from oven and set aside for cutting later.

Creating the sauce:
Add butter, garlic, shallots, peach and brandy to the darkened pan. Whip the ingredients until they blend into a sauce.

Drizzle the sauce on a plate. Cut cooked veal into inch medallions and place on plate on top of the sauce.

Add cooked vegetables: asparagus, broccoli, potatoes, carrots, red pepper and garnish with a leaf of fresh basil and a sprig of thyme.

Chef Recommended Wine

Argiano
Brunello di Montalcino

Glossary of Wine Terms

Reserva: A Spanish term for a red wine that has spent at least three years in barrels and bottles before release.

Reserve: A largely American term indicating a wine of higher quality; it has no legal meaning.

Rhône: A river in southwest France surrounded by villages producing wines mostly from Syrah; the name of the wine-producing valley in France.

Riddling: The process of rotating Champagne bottles in order to shift sediment toward the cork.

Riesling: Along with Chardonnay, one of the top white grapes in the world; most popular in Germany, Alsace and Austria.

Rioja: A well-known region in Spain known for traditional red wines made from the Tempranillo grape.

Rosé: French for "pink," and used to describe a category of refreshing wines that are pink in color but are made from red grapes.

Sancerre: An area in the Loire Valley known mostly for wines made from Sauvignon Blanc.

Sangiovese: A red grape native to Tuscany; the base grape for Chianti, Brunello di Montalcino, Morellino di Scansano and others.

2001

Argiano
Brunello di
Montalcino

Full red. Highly complex aromas of medicinal black cherry, mocha, licorice and black olive, with a roasted aspect and a whiff of celery seed. Sweet, densely packed and concentrated, with lush, seamless dark fruit flavors spreading out to saturate the palate. A big, firmly structured Brunello that finishes with ripe tannins and intriguing hints of iron and peat.

50 Recipes & glass of Wine

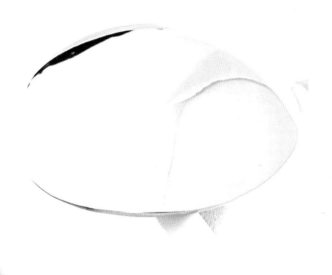

Zuppa di Pesce

Ingredients

- 3 lbs. assorted fish: squid, octopus, shrimps, scallops, clams or mussels

- 3 tomatoes

- lemon(optional)

- 3 cloves garlic

- 2 sprigs parsley

- Salt & pepper

- 2 tablespoons olive oil

DIRECTIONS

Gut and clean all the fish. Fillet the fish with bone and cut the squid and octopus into pieces while reserving the heads and bones.

Bring 6 qts. water to boil in a large pot; add the tomatoes, the fish bones and heads, including the shrimps' heads. Cook for 2 hours, then cool and pass through a fine sieve. Bring this poaching liquid back to a simmer and start adding the fish, one at a time, in order of cooking time. Cook until all the fish are done.

Prepare and sauté the garlic and parsley; add to the fish stew and remove from heat. Finish with lemon juice, place in a large serving platter and serve with toasted country bread.

Chef Recommended Wine

Kris
Pinot Grigio

Glossary of Wine Terms

Sauternes: A sweet Bordeaux white wine made from botrytized Sémillon and Sauvignon Blanc.

Sauvignon Blanc: A white grape planted throughout the world; increasingly the signature wine of New Zealand.

Sémillon: A plump white grape popular in Bordeaux and Australia; the base for Sauternes.

Sherry: A fortified wine from a denominated region in southwest Spain; styles include fino, Manzanilla, oloroso and amontillado.

Shiraz: The Australian name for Syrah; also used in South Africa and sparingly in the U.S.

Silky: A term used to describe a wine with an especially smooth mouthfeel.

Solera: The Spanish system of blending wines of different ages to create a harmonious end product; a stack of barrels holding wines of various ages.

Sommelier: Technically a wine steward, but one potentially with a great degree of wine knowledge as well as a diploma of sorts in wine studies.

Spicy: A term used to describe certain aromas and flavors that may be sharp, woody or sweet.

2004

*Kris
Pinot Grigio*

A beautiful floral nose reveals hints of honeyed lemon, orange rind, & pears. Crisp, light to medium-bodied, refreshing and impeccably well-made.

recipes & glass of Wine

Veal with Mushrooms & Yellow Pepper

Ingredients

- 1 small chopped onion
- 1 carrot peeled & chopped
- 1 stalk of celery, chopped
- 1 cup fresh whole mushrooms
- 4 yellow peppers
- salt & pepper
- butter
- 1 teaspoon chopped parsely
- 1 small clove of garlic, minced
- 1/4 cup dry white wine
- 4 Veal Steaks , 5 oz. each

DIRECTIONS

Sauté garlic, onion, carrot, and celery in butter until onion is limp.

Sauté and brown fresh whole mushrooms and yellow pepper.

Flatten veal steak to 1/16" thick (17mm) Sprinkle both sides with salt pepper, and flour.

In a large skillet, melt butter and oil; sauté veal over medium heat about 3 minutes per side until golden brown.

Add all vegetables with the steak and put the dry white wine and let cook for a few minutes.

Sprinkle all with fresh parsely.

Chef Recommended Wine

Salviano
Rosso Turlo

Glossary of Wine Terms

Split: A quarter-bottle of wine; a single-serving bottle equal to 175 milliliters.

Steely: A term used to describe an extremely crisp, acidic wine that was not aged in barrels.

Stemmy: A term used to describe harsh, green characteristics in a wine.

Super Tuscan: A red wine from Tuscany that is not made in accordance with established DOC rules; often a blended wine of superior quality containing Cabernet Sauvignon and/or Merlot.

Syrah: A red grape planted extensively in the Rhône Valley of France, Australia and elsewhere; a spicy, full and tannic wine that usually requires aging before it can be enjoyed.

Table Wine: A term used to describe wines of between 10 and 14 percent alcohol; in Europe, table wines are those that are made outside of regulated regions or by unapproved methods.

Tannins: Phenolic compounds that exist in most plants; in grapes, tannins are found primarily in the skins and pits; tannins are astringent and provide structure to a wine; over time tannins die off, making wines less harsh.

Tempranillo: The most popular red grape in Spain; common in Rioja and Ribera del Duero.

2003

Salviano Rosso Turlo

Good, rich pompegranate color. Complex & intense aroma with hints of jame & mature fruit. Very soft & long lasting with good body. Excellent wine for aging.

50 Recipes & glass of Wine

Marinated Grilled Shrimp Salad

Ingredients

- 1 lb. lg. large shrimp, cut in half
- 1 c. olive oil
- 1/2 c. white wine
- 1 tbsp. lemon juice
- 2-3 cloves garlic, chopped fine
- 1/4 cup balsamic vinegar
- 1/4 cup fresh chopped parsley
- 1 lb. spring mix salad

DIRECTIONS

Wash shrimp in cold water and drain.

Cut shrimp in half.

Prepare marinade. Marinate in large bowl at least 2 hours. Arrange on rack and grill over medium heat about 5 minutes each side.

Place spring mix on plate arrange the half shrimp all around.

Pour remaining marinate sauce over salad and shrimp.

Chef Recommended Wine

La Scolca
Gavi Di Gavi
Black Label

Glossary of Wine Terms

Terroir: A French term for the combination of soil, climate and all other factors that influence the ultimate character of a wine.

Tokay: A dessert wine made in Hungary from dried Furmint grapes.

Trocken: German for "dry".

Varietal: A wine made from just one grape type and named after that grape; the opposite of a blend.

Veneto: A large wine-producing region in northern Italy.

Vin Santo: Sweet wine from Tuscany made from late-harvest Trebbiano and Malvasia grapes.

Viticulture: The science and business of growing wine grapes.

Vintage: A particular year in the wine business; a specific harvest.

Viognier: A fragrant, powerful white grape grown in the Rhône Valley of France and elsewhere.

Yeast: Organisms that issue enzymes that trigger the fermentation process; yeasts can be natural or commercial.

Yield: The amount of grapes harvested in a particular year.

Zinfandel: A popular grape in California of disputed origin; scientists say it is related to grapes in Croatia and southern Italy.

2004

La Scolca Gavi Di Gavi Black Label

Pale straw color, with delicate greenish highlights. Intense fruit and floral fragrance. On the palate it is strongly typical of Gavi: fruity and flinty with notes of almonds, hazelnuts & walnuts lingering in the finish.

INDEX

INDEX

INDEX